Advance praise for *New Job, New You*

"Is it time to follow your passion? Spend m̶o̶r̶e̶ ̶t̶i̶m̶e̶ ̶w̶i̶t̶h̶ ̶y̶o̶u̶r̶ family? Walk through the job tran̶s̶i̶t̶i̶o̶n̶ ̶p̶r̶o̶c̶e̶s̶s̶ ̶w̶i̶t̶h̶ ̶A̶l̶e̶xandra Levit's *New Job, New You*. ̶B̶y̶ ̶t̶h̶e̶ ̶e̶n̶d̶ ̶o̶f̶ ̶t̶h̶i̶s̶ ̶i̶n̶s̶i̶g̶htful book, you'll be prepared to ̶t̶a̶c̶k̶l̶e̶ ̶y̶o̶u̶r̶ ̶n̶e̶x̶t̶ ̶j̶ob."
—**Marshall Goldsmith, au̶t̶h̶o̶r̶ ̶o̶f̶ ̶W̶h̶a̶t̶ ̶G̶o̶t̶ ̶Y̶o̶u̶ ̶H̶e̶r̶e̶ *You There***

"Career change is scary. Ale̶x̶a̶n̶d̶r̶a̶ ̶s̶h̶o̶w̶s̶ ̶y̶o̶u̶ ̶h̶o̶w̶ ̶t̶o̶ ̶f̶e̶ar and do it anyway. *New Job, New You* is f̶u̶l̶l̶ ̶o̶f̶ inspiring stories and smart advice for anyone who longs for a more fulfilling career. I will confidently recommend this wonderful book to my career coaching clients."
—**Pamela Skillings, author of *Escape from Corporate America***

"Alexandra Levit is *the* career guru of our times! Part adventure ride, part career guidebook, *New Job, New You* is outstanding and could not come at a better time for the many Americans who suffer work-related frustrations." —**Lisa Haneberg, author of *Two Weeks to a Breakthrough***

"Changing careers is in vogue, but what's missing for most people is the reason to do it in the first place, as well as the step-by-step actions required to make it happen. *New Job, New You* explores the journeys of accomplished career changers at various life stages and instructs readers how to replicate their success." —**Penelope Trunk, author of *Brazen Careerist***

"This well-sourced guide can help nearly every working adult, since we all entertain thoughts of switching careers at some points in our lives. *New Job, New You* could become the wisest investment for reshaping your professional life!" —**Tom Musbach, editor, Yahoo! HotJobs**

"Written by seasoned career expert Alexandra Levit, *New Job, New You* is the perfect book for people who feel lost and are looking for a change. It sprinkles in just the right amount of motivation and practical advice to get you off the dime." —**Cali Ressler, co-author of *Why Work Sucks and How to Fix It***

"At a time when the future is uncertain and career reinvention is widespread, *New Job, New You* has the secret formula for opening your eyes and empowering you to make a difference in your life."
—**Dan Schawbel, author of *Me 2.0***

"The personal stories of how different individuals made their own career change are perhaps the jewels of this book. People learn through the example of others. *New Job, New You* offers practical and real-world

advice about taking charge of the career you want. Anyone thinking about reinventing themselves would do well to read this book."
—**Chris Russell, founder of JobRadio.FM**

"Career changes aren't easy, and now thanks to Alexandra Levit, no one has to undertake one blindly. In *New Job, New You,* Levit provides both interesting and varied examples of successful career changers interspersed with inspirational and practical advice. A must-read for anyone seeking a career change in this difficult economy."
—**Diane K. Danielson, CEO of DowntownWomensClub.com**

"I can't wait to give this book to everyone I know who's whined about hating their job or wondered how to pick themselves up after a devastating layoff. Alexandra Levit takes the guesswork and fear out of creating your own self-styled career, even in a shaky economic climate. The checklists, resources, and in-your-face quizzes alone are worth the cover price." —**Michelle Goodman, author of *My So-Called Freelance Life* and *The Anti 9-to-5 Guide***

"In *New Job, New You,* Alexandra Levit provides a wealth of information, ideas and inspiration for career changers in a wide variety of situations. This book combines Levit's expert guidance with courageous examples of real people who will motivate readers to take the leap into new careers of their own. I highly recommend it!" —**Lindsey Pollak, author of *Getting from College to Career***

"*New Job, New You* is not just another career book—it is a must-have resource for individuals at professional crossroads. Alexandra Levit combines thorough research, years of career coaching experience, and a fresh perspective to the topic of career transition." —**Christine Hassler, author of *20 Something Manifesto***

"Alexandra Levit's *New Job, New You* should be handed out in unemployment offices, college career centers, and chamber of commerce branches across the country. Anyone who dreams of starting a new career, but who is afraid to take that first step, will find Levit's book priceless." —**Maria Pascucci, founder and president of Campus Calm**

"A timely, comprehensive, and no-fluff guide that answers the all-important questions of career change. If you've ever wanted to reinvent yourself but haven't known where to start, read this book."
—**Chris Guillebeau, author of the blog The Art of Non-Conformity**

NEW JOB, NEW YOU

NEW JOB, NEW YOU

A GUIDE TO
REINVENTING YOURSELF
IN A BRIGHT NEW CAREER

ALEXANDRA LEVIT

BALLANTINE BOOKS TRADE PAPERBACKS · NEW YORK

For Jonah, who was born as this book began.

A Ballantine Books Trade Paperback Original

Published in the United States by Ballantine Books, an imprint of The Random House Publishing Group, a division of Random House, Inc., New York.

BALLANTINE and colophon are registered trademarks of Random House, Inc.

Library of Congress Cataloging-in-Publication Data

Levit, Alexandra.
New job, new you: a guide to reinventing yourself in a bright new career / Alexandra Levit.
p. cm.
"A Ballantine Books Trade Paperback original."
Includes bibliographical references.
ISBN 978-0-345-50880-5 (pbk.)
1. Career changes. 2. Job hunting. 3. Self-actualization (Psychology) I. Title.
HF5384.L483 2009
650.14—dc22 2009036892

Printed in the United States of America

www.ballantinebooks.com

2 4 6 8 9 7 5 3 1

Book design by Adrianna Sutton

Foreword

BY STEPHEN R. COVEY

This is a truly amazing book. You ask me why it's so amazing? First of all, it's extremely timely and relevant. It starts with the mind, heart, and need of the reader, and the stories are real. It also is multidimensional, in that it focuses on the seven motivations that influence career decisions: family, independence, learning, money, passion, setback, and talent. Each of these motivational sections contains five real stories that magnificently illustrate the points being made. It also includes Alexandra Levit's very wise counsel about preparing to put the change to work. Each preparation is uniquely suited to the nature of the motivation being developed. Every section includes a resource toolkit, book suggestions, and many extremely practical ideas on how to put the change to work.

I've always believed that we possess four unique human gifts, or endowments, that animals do not possess: self-awareness, imagination, conscience, and willpower. Every story here embodies these four endowments or gifts—not in theoretical or philosophical terms, but in very practical things to do.

We live in a new economy that is moving from the Industrial Age, top-down, command-and-control, hierarchical model to the Knowledge Worker Age of empowerment and courage and creativity. We also live at a difficult recessionary time, but that does not mean we are fundamentally a product of our environment. We are not victims of circumstances. We are the creative force of our own lives. Every story given in this book beautifully illustrates and motivates us to become this creative force and to avoid the metastasizing cancers of victimism and co-dependency.

When you read these stories, your sense of creativity, courage, self confidence, and business savvy will profoundly increase. It will be enormously encouraging to you, particularly in this new economy and difficult recessionary period.

Frankly, I've never found a book quite like it, in terms of its encouragement, wisdom, practicality, and sheer enlightenment. I will recommend this book to all who are stuck in their careers and who want to do something different. I will recommend it to people who need to grow in self-reflection and self-awareness, in the use of their imagination, in consulting their conscience regarding their passion and talent, and in exercising their independent will to make these good things happen.

I hope you will soon see for yourself why I am so amazed by this book. How motivating and enlightening! I can see also why Alexandra Levit's other books, *They Don't Teach Corporate in College*, *How'd You Score That Gig?*, and *Success for Hire*, have been so successful.

Contents

Introduction

It used to be that only celebrities like Madonna reinvented themselves. But this is the twenty-first century, and the United States Bureau of Labor Statistics predicts that the average American will have about nine jobs between the ages of eighteen and thirty-two. Some have taken this trend a step further. They have changed not just their jobs but their fields, and have successfully supported themselves in different careers over a period of several years.

I'm proud to say that I'm a card-carrying member of this group. I started off my career as a public relations account executive in New York City. I chose PR because I had studied communications in college and liked it. I also wanted to make a lot of money and live in the big city. When the country celebrated the dot-com boom, I delved into interactive marketing, and after I received an opportunity to work five minutes away from my new condo in Long Island, I returned to traditional PR. My experiences working for a global communications agency and a Fortune 500 software firm taught me not only the mechanics of publicity, but also how the business world operated and what young people needed to know to be victorious there.

My second act started mostly by accident. The transition from college to career was anything but easy, and when things finally started moving in the right direction, I wanted to share what I'd learned with other twenty-something employees. A would-be fiction writer at the time, I was familiar with the process of pitching a book, so I went out with the idea for *They Don't Teach Corporate in College:*

A Twenty-Something's Guide to the Business World. The book was acquired by a small publisher, and I was fortunate that it sold well. I was doing better in my marketing communications career than I ever had before, but the next thing I knew I was being asked to write for respected media outlets and travel around the country to speak about workplace issues facing young employees. The success of *They Don't Teach Corporate in College,* which was originally intended as a side project, had established my platform as a twenty-something career expert.

Other books followed, and with the birth of my son in 2008, I finally completed the transition from PR VP to author, speaker, and consultant. I couldn't be happier and more satisfied, for my job now allows me to make a tangible difference in people's lives every day. Although I mastered many aspects of the PR profession during my time in the business world, I couldn't necessarily say that my colleagues and clients were personally and professionally better off for having worked with me in that capacity.

Twenty- and thirty-somethings (or members of Generations X and Y) who hear about my journey are understandably curious about it. Because young professionals so often find themselves on career autopilot as a result of impromptu decisions made in college or shortly thereafter, career change is one of the hottest topics today. In fact, according to a recent CareerBuilder survey of more than 5,700 young workers, more than a third of respondents (35 percent) said they were interested in making a career change, and in my experience as a career expert, career change is one of the most frequently requested speaking topics on college campuses and at association conferences.

On the whole, members of Generations X and Y are looking to adapt their work to the lifestyle changes they're making as they mature. However, they understand that it's hard to do—especially now. The damaged economy and the poor job market have resulted in extreme competition in all types of fields, including those that weren't considered desirable before. In *New Job, New You,* I'll show you how you can stand out from millions of others with the same goals and aspirations. For example, in many of the chapters I'll address how to acquire the right combination of education and experience for your new field, how to create an inner circle of contacts and mentors who can propel you forward, and how to move the needle a little bit at a time so that you stay productive and sane while your competition is giving up around you. You'll come out on top because you'll have established yourself as the total package: a person who is ahead of the game emotionally and financially as well as professionally.

When I announced on my website that I would be working on *New Job, New You,* I received dozens of enthusiastic emails. People wanted a book that would get to the heart of what makes people take the plunge into a new field, a book that included the formula for doing it successfully despite significant societal obstacles. As I conducted my research, I discovered that career changers have several common motivations for their decisions, and therefore selected these motivations as the book's unifying theme. They are:

- **Family:** When true work/life balance becomes a necessity
- **Independence:** When you've been bitten by the entrepreneurial bug
- **Learning:** When your bookish, curious side takes over
- **Money:** When an increase in earning potential is on the horizon
- **Passion:** When you yearn to do what you love with all of your heart
- **Setback:** When one door closes, another one opens
- **Talent:** When you're too good at something not to give it a shot

Each chapter includes stories of five people who began their careers in one line of work, and, while in their twenties or thirties, experienced one or more of these motivations. Moving forward, they used their existing skills and networking abilities, as well as the education available to them, to make dramatic and courageous transitions. Throughout, the book provides mini-assessments, exercises, resource toolkits, and expert advice for how you can follow similar trajectories.

New Job, New You is about harnessing your own motivations to execute changes that will enhance your work satisfaction. Let's start with a quiz that will help you determine if a career transformation is something you are seriously ready to consider.

☞ Assessment: Should You Make a Career Change?

Please select "True" or "False" in response to the following statements.

1. You feel that you are a different person now than when you first started your career.

    True   False

2. When you consider your long-term life plan, your current career path doesn't match up with where you want to go.

    True   False

3. If you didn't need the money, you could walk away from your field tomorrow and never look back.

    True   False

4. Your work often feels frustrating and unnatural to you.

    True   False

5. Your current field doesn't support the lifestyle you would like to have for yourself or your family.

    True   False

6. Looking into the future, you see technology or another development rendering your job obsolete.

    True   False

7. You have reached the highest level in your career that you can reasonably aspire to, and you don't see additional opportunities for growth in the foreseeable future.

    True   False

8. You would like to get another job, but you're afraid to rock the boat since your field is small and positions are difficult to come by.

    True   False

9. You've wanted to pursue a certain type of career for a long time, but circumstances forced you into something else that never quite fit as well.

    True   False

10. The work you do on a daily basis doesn't interest you, and you constantly find yourself stealing glances at the clock.
    True   False

11. You've spent hours on the Internet researching alternative lines of work.
    True   False

12. Your current career doesn't make good use of your education and unique set of skills and talents.
    True   False

13. You've had the opportunity to take a different position in your field, but you don't see how it would make a difference.
    True   False

14. The only thing that's appealing about your job is your co-workers.
    True   False

15. You can't remember what made you choose your industry in the first place.
    True   False

16. You know in your heart that you need to move on to a new field, but you haven't because you resist change or lack experience.
    True   False

17. Your field doesn't afford opportunities to explore new directions and address fresh challenges.
    True   False

18. The decision to go into your current field wasn't your own and you find it hard to understand why others rave about it.
    True   False

19. You've gone on job interviews in your field where you've been told that you are overqualified, or were asked to accept a salary much lower than your experience warrants.
    True   False

20. Although you've lost your passion for your work, you are worried that no one will value you at the bottom rung of a new career.
    True   False

21. You don't believe that your current field allows you to contribute to society or that your work matters, and this bothers you.
    True   False

22. If you were to give a current college student an informational interview about your field, it would be difficult to be positive.
    True   False

23. You've been told that you need to acquire additional education or training to keep up in your field, and you haven't been motivated to do this.
    True   False

24. After a recent vacation, or an event that got you thinking more about the purpose of life, you returned to work with regret.
    True   False

25. After years in the traditional workforce, you've finally realized that you won't be truly satisfied unless you can be your own boss.
    True   False

Add up the total number of "True" and "False" answers and score your quiz according to this key.

👎 **Five or more "True" answers:** You probably sensed this already, but your current career just isn't doing it for you anymore. Perhaps you stay in your field because it's easier, or because you're afraid. The forthcoming chapters will introduce you to possibilities you might not have considered, and alternate paths that have been taken by people just like you.

👍 **Less than five "True" answers:** Perhaps you are already in the field that's right for you, but there are some aspects of your current job situation that aren't ideal. Depending on your motivations, this book will provide ways to adapt your existing career to your current needs.

NEW JOB, NEW YOU

Family

The only rock I know that stays steady,
the only institution I know that works is the family.

—Lee Iacocca, business magnate

As a young professional, I was always told by my mentors that I shouldn't make a decision about whether to reconfigure my career to accommodate children until the first one arrived. "You can never tell how you're going to feel or what you'll want to do," they cautioned. Yet somehow I knew that I would always want to work without shipping my kids off to a day-care center eighty hours a week. So in my mid-twenties, little by little, I started creating a career that would allow me to be home a few days a week, with the ability to juggle my work and family lives as I saw fit. By the time my son was born, I was able to support myself as a writer and speaker. I work in my home office three days a week, and spend the other two at playgroups and music classes.

You might associate a schedule like mine with self-employment, but the workplace is shifting in this regard. As Phyllis Furman recently reported in the New York *Daily News*, global consulting behemoth Ernst & Young provides a flexible work arrangement to 10 percent of its approximately three thousand New York area employees. Also, when American Express learned in a Center for Work-Life Policy survey that one-quarter of women worry they could hurt their careers by asking for flexibility, the company allowed select employees to customize their schedules to work twenty-one hours a week without negatively affecting their shot at advancement.

Some fields, however, simply don't permit individuals to put their families first, and this is a major reason that workers who are concerned about children, spouses, and even aging parents decide to change careers. In this chapter, you'll meet some inspiring individuals who took their schedules into their own hands and custom-created careers that are compatible with spending precious time with loved ones. They are some of the happiest people I came across while working on this book, and they are as proud of their ability to achieve balance as they are of their professional endeavors. I'll close with some guidance about how to adjust your own career—either by transitioning to a more family-friendly field or by taking advantage of new policies where you are—in order to make the people waiting at home a higher priority in your life.

Leslie
From High-Tech Saleswoman to Novelist

A high-achieving student in the Wharton undergraduate program at the University of Pennsylvania, Leslie was assured a bright future. Shortly before graduation, minority recruiters from Xerox Corporation attended a large job fair in Philadelphia and literally picked Leslie out of a lineup. "I chose a career in high-tech sales because I had monster student loans and the pay was the best," Leslie says.

Over the next several years, Leslie sold "big-box" equipment for Xerox, Hewlett-Packard, and Digital Equipment Corporation—companies with the most professionally recognized sales forces in the country. "I learned almost military-like discipline, how to have a thick skin when it comes to rejection, and how to understand business models, profits, margins, and ROI [return on investment]," she says. "I also figured out how to sell based on listening to what customers were really saying they needed, and by the end, I could sell *anything*."

Leslie, married and with a newborn, was a supermom. The stress took its toll, but Leslie continued on her path as a driven sales executive until her daughter was in an unthinkable accident at her day-care center. "My six-month-old was left in a room with an ironing board and a hot iron," Leslie recalls. "She pulled on the cord and spilled scalding hot water on herself. I left my job that day and went to sit vigil at the hospital. She lost three fingers and had seventeen surgeries."

These were the days before the Family and Medical Leave Act, and representatives from Leslie's company—she dubs them the "Men in Black"—came to visit her and "nicely" laid her off. "There I was, unemployed, on the verge of divorce, with no legal settlement because the day-care provider didn't have insurance," she says. "The day I looked down at my helpless, burned little baby with third-degree wounds all down her left arm and hand, I decided that no matter what, I wasn't leaving my child in the hands of anyone else."

Financially, though, Leslie was in trouble. "I had been making six figures, and then, nothing. It was like doing a high-wire act and suddenly realizing that there's no net," she says. "I liquidated everything I had, bled out savings. I started a gift basket company, did people's résumés, wrote grants, and hustled a bit as a consultant." Then Leslie saw an ad in a magazine for a short-story contest. The winner received $2,500 in prize money. "My goal was very short-term—write the damn story and win."

Leslie never submitted that short story because it was too long, but she kept working on it and before long, she had a book. Without Leslie's knowledge, her girlfriends sent the finished manuscript to publishers, and before long she was offered her first deal. She had found a fulfilling career that she could have as a stay-at-home mom, and she jumped on it. Leslie began writing like there was no tomorrow, eventually penning more than thirty novels and eleven novellas in a wide range of genres from romance to crime suspense. She recently won *Essence* magazine's Storyteller of the Year Award and transitioned into the hot new genre of paranormal fiction with her twelve-book Vampire Huntress Legend series.

Leslie's experiences caring for her daughter have infused her writing with compassion and empathy. "My child was badly hurt, but she is relatively normal save the loss of part of her hand. I saw people grieving because their children were dead or worse, so horribly disfigured or mentally damaged that there was no end to the nightmare," she says. "I also realized that the deck is stacked against people who are experiencing hardship, and that you're not necessarily a deadbeat because you can't pay your bills. We are all close to being a paycheck or two from homelessness, and when I see people begging in the street now, I'm not so quick to walk by them."

Leslie, who writes under several pen names (www.leslieesdaile banks.com), feels blessed to have survived what she terms a frightening, sobering, and humbling journey that has resulted in greater accomplishment than she ever imagined. "I have the best job in the world. I'm a full-time author and I get paid to create entertaining stories," she says. "I work at my own pace and am home for my daughter whenever she needs me. I go to a lot of great conferences, but when I'm not traveling, I keep the same schedule: see my child off to school in the morning, walk the dog, answer email, and begin editing. I end my day when my daughter comes home so that we can eat dinner together, and then when she starts her homework, I sit down and let my creativity flow."

Many people write novels, but few make enough money at it to be able to stay at home and watch their children grow. Leslie credits her endurance, discipline, and a strong sense of her own spirituality. "I can't tell you how often I have conversations with God," she says. To those who are looking to change careers, she advises, "Start now before you are forced to. Do a little bit every night to chip away at the task. And begin your new career as a sideline to your regular job. That way, you'll have a trial period to gain strength and financial stability before you jump ship."

J.B.
From Automotive Marketer to Toy Producer

As a Detroit native, it's no surprise that thirty-nine-year-old J.B. got his start in the car business. Shortly after graduating from John Carroll University with a degree in marketing, he went to work for the Caribiner Group, where he coordinated corporate meetings for large automotive clients. "These were multimillion-dollar productions in which automotive executives would introduce new car models to their sales forces and dealers," explains J.B. "It was a great experience on many fronts. I got to be a part of the inner workings of some of the most famous companies, and I learned the essentials of communication by working with some of the best speechwriters, coaches, and presentation creators out there."

J.B. wanted to expand his marketing horizons beyond meeting planning, however, so he took a job at DMB&B, a more traditional firm that represented Cadillac and Pontiac. Responsible for catalogs and dealership collateral materials, as a young twenty-something J.B. found himself managing multifaceted projects. "I worked with the client engineers on catalog content, as well as our art directors, copywriters, graphic designers, and print production staff," he says. "It was a challenge figuring out how to get the most out of all of these people."

J.B. spent the next few years continuing to market cars. His job at DMB&B was followed by a direct marketing position at advertising powerhouse McCann-Erickson, and then by a role as a marketing manager at a division of General Motors. Of the latter job, he says: "I was exposed to so much because the company was exploring different areas of growth, and backed by GM we had the resources to get things done. It was fantastic… that is, until it got too big and too bureaucratic."

At the age of twenty-eight, J.B. married his college sweetheart, Michele, with whom he'd had a long-distance relationship. They began building their family soon afterward, welcoming daughter Anna and son Konrad. "There's something about having children that makes you picture your life down the road," says J.B. "I knew I didn't want to be marketing cars when my kids were in college. I wanted to be on my own, and to be able to participate in my kids' lives while they were growing up."

J.B. decided that the best path to entrepreneurship would be a master's degree of business administration from Babson College, near Boston. "I needed a new network and the right MBA program could help me develop that," he says. J.B. was making a career change in part because of his family, and his family was what saw him through the obstacles. "Without their emotional support and day-to-day help, I never would have made it through the long road of GMAT testing, applications, choosing where to go, selling the house and most everything in it, moving, and downgrading our lifestyle."

Indeed, the pressure was on. J.B. and Michele had two more children, and J.B. felt compelled to make sure the family was comfortable financially as soon as he finished school. The couple was also devastated by the sudden deaths of two of their siblings, including the sister to whom J.B. was closest. "These losses further cemented my decision to pursue the dream of having my own business. After all, you never know what's going to happen. We could all be gone tomorrow."

In the Babson MBA program, J.B. met Antonio Turco-Rivas, a classmate who shared J.B.'s desire to involve his family in doing what he loved. Both being parents, J.B. and Antonio realized that home is one of the key environments where children play and learn, and they saw a need to improve play furniture. J.B. and Antonio sponsored research with the Rhode Island School of Design, and the result was their new company's flagship product, the P'kolino Play Table. Before they knew it, the two had finished their degrees, moved to South Florida to be closer to their extended families, and were getting their children's input on new designs for chairs, benches, desks, and storage containers.

Today, J.B. is in charge of the product development and marketing functions for P'kolino (www.pkolino.com). "I've always been a closet engineer, so I love being hands-on, working with the prototypes," he says. "And things are going well. We've recently started working with large clients like Babies 'R' Us, and moving many of our products overseas. But Antonio and I, we're never satisfied. We want P'kolino to be a household name."

What J.B. is satisfied with, though, is his lifestyle. "I'm in total control of my career, and that means no more useless face time—feeling like you have to be in the office even if your work is done," he says. "I'm in a situation where I can keep on top of things while making time to take my kids to school and socialize with the other parents. I never have to apologize to anyone for making my family a priority."

J.B. encourages others to acknowledge that what is important to your family should have an impact on the career you choose. "You can create any type of life you want, but it will often require stepping out of your comfort zone," he says. "Just remember that the fear of regret is stronger than the fear of failure."

Erica
From Television Ad Manager to "Mom-preneur"

Erica always had a special hobby that wasn't shared by other kids her age. Transfixed by commercials instead of television shows, Erica spoke in taglines as a child. She spent her teen years shadowing her uncle, who was an art director at an advertising agency in Houston and in college she worked at radio and television stations. "I got an internship building content and advertising opportunities at an America Online subsite, the Family Travel Network," says Erica, now thirty-three. "But when I began looking for a full-time job in advertising or marketing I found few options. Then, one day I heard that a local radio station was recruiting telemarketers to staff a new phone center for listener research. I impressed the team and was offered an account executive job for one of their newest radio stations, WRBT-FM in Harrisburg, Pennsylvania."

Erica had never considered working in sales, but she figured she'd take the job to learn as much as she could and position herself for a promotion into the marketing department. Ironically, though, Erica quickly discovered she had genuine sales skill—and that she hated the radio business. She accepted a sales job in television at the CBS affiliate in Harrisburg and immediately felt at home. "I studied my clients, their competitors, and their messaging," she explains. "I knew that if I could create campaigns that were solution-based rather than just negotiate spot schedules, I would earn business."

In the two years Erica worked for CBS, she got married and gave birth to her first daughter. The new family relocated to Washington, D.C., where Erica continued her television sales career as an account executive with WUSA-TV, Gannett's CBS station, and then WRC-TV, the NBC affiliate. While at NBC, Erica grew her account list and became one of the top billers at the station. But despite her success, she felt herself slipping back into the part of the job she disliked—negotiating rates and spot schedules and making deals over the phone. She yearned to return to her solution-driven approach to sales, where she was part of the planning process and not just someone who appeared at the end to configure a placement.

Erica stepped up her efforts to take advantage of new business opportunities that included station sponsorships and customized programs for TV, events, and the Internet, and her results landed her a promotion. Then, about a year later, Erica got a call from her sister station in Philadelphia. "They were creating a new marketing management position, and I drove up for the interview," Erica says. "On my way back to D.C., the vice president called and offered me the position. I was so excited I almost drove off the highway. I was twenty-seven years old and I had my dream job—a marketing manager at an NBC affiliate in the fourth-largest market in the country."

Erica called her husband to tell him the news, but unfortunately, he didn't share her enthusiasm. "He didn't want to move and told me to decline the position," she says. "Eventually he relented, but this was the first time I was faced with the reality that what was best for my career wasn't necessarily what was best for my family." Up in Philadelphia, Erica focused on becoming an all-around marketing pro, working with the national and regional sales teams as well as the news, interactive, and community departments to sell sponsorships and create creative, branded campaigns around them.

When Erica gave birth to her second daughter and returned to work after her maternity leave, she was tasked with managing a business development department in addition to her existing responsibilities. "I was under intense pressure to get it right and show results quickly," Erica remembers. "In the first year, my team generated three million dollars in new business, but we needed to double that. It seemed no matter how much I gave, they needed more."

One random June afternoon, Erica left work early to have dinner with her kids, something she only did a few times a year. "I will never forget that day," she says. "I walked into the backyard, expecting to hear my daughters screaming 'Mommy's home!' Instead I found my husband playing in the pool with the girls. They were laughing and having the greatest time. As I stood there watching them in my suit, I realized I was going to work every day to afford a life I wasn't even a part of. My girls were eight and almost two, and I hardly knew them. I had to rethink my life."

Together with a friend, Erica brainstormed the idea for a website that would help moms find local services they needed, complete with ratings and reviews from other moms. When they talked to their prospective audience and got a resounding response, Erica closed her eyes, held her breath, and quit her job. Originally financed by Erica's friend and now business partner, MomSpace (www.mom space.com) is thriving—but not without some bumps along the way. "I thought that since I knew how to make money, the rest would fall into place, but suddenly I was struggling to understand the ins and outs of the information technology industry," Erica says. "I thought I could just hire certain skill sets, but boy was I wrong. You can't hire anyone unless you know enough to realize what you need." She has also had to overcome the skepticism of her former clients and colleagues. "When I'd talk about tightening the purse strings in order to make a go of the business, they thought I'd lost it and would squeal, 'What, no Louis Vuitton?' They all wondered how long it would take me to come back. Well, they're still waiting."

Erica now creates her schedule around her children. In the morning, she gets them ready for the day, and then depending on circumstances, she'll work from home or go into the office. Her work responsibilities vary. "I might work with the content team to make sure we have relevant articles on the site, talk with office administration to see that invoicing has been done properly, take calls from potential investors, or work on strategy with my partner," she says. Able to eat with her family whenever she likes, Erica feels both stressed out and exhilarated by her new career. "It's a totally different ball game when you own the issues in every department, but I couldn't be more excited about what we're building."

Erica urges would-be family men and women to be realistic. "There may be times in your new situation when you actually see your family less. With any major life change there's a period of adjustment, so don't second-guess your decision because it's harder than you thought," she says. Reflecting on her own transition, Erica adds, "I learned the importance of a strong sense of self. It's so easy to get lost in this world, judging your worth by your job title or pay-check. I now have a clear picture of the mother, wife, and woman I want to be. I hold on to that every day."

Lisa Marie
From Bank Teller to Federal Law Enforcement Officer to Leadership Company President

Thirty-nine-year-old Lisa Marie hails from a working-class neighbor-hood in Allentown, Pennsylvania. Going to college wasn't common in her family, but Lisa Marie always wanted a job that wasn't typi-cally open to women. "I grew up watching police shows and *Murder, She Wrote* with my grandparents, and one of my mom's friends sug-gested I check out criminal justice as a career," Lisa Marie says. "It appealed to the protector in me, so I pursued a bachelor of science at the University of Scranton."

As she got closer to graduation, however, summers working at Arby's diminished Lisa Marie's career ambition. While she was still in school, she got a job working the shredder at the People First Credit Union in Allentown. "After I finished my degree, I went to work there as a teller," she says. "It wasn't really a career choice, it was more that I wanted to eat. But I started worrying that I'd be there forever and never use my degree. Banking might have been safe, but if I didn't make a change now, when would I?"

Lisa Marie decided that she wanted to see the world, so she hit the library and researched government jobs that involved law enforcement and travel. After applying and taking an aptitude test, Lisa Marie qualified to work at the U.S. Customs and Border Pro-tection agency. Her first position was with the marine department and her main responsibility was to "clear the ships" and ensure all of the paperwork was in order for large vessels entering the Port of Newark/New York from international waters. Next, Lisa Marie went to work for the Contraband Enforcement Team, where she spent many a hot and sweaty day looking for narcotics in containers of everything from African wooden paddles to frozen sharks.

A third role with Outbound Enforcement involved inspecting

cargo leaving the United States to check for illegally smuggled funds. "Despite my experience, I was basically forced into a lesser position because I was a woman," Lisa Marie relates. "But you know what, I learned a lot. In scheduling overtime, I was a neutral party dealing with people's money. There was so much infighting about who was going to get off when, and it was a struggle to pay attention and listen to people. I realized that things don't always work out the way we want and we still have to make the best of them."

Meanwhile, Lisa Marie had gotten involved in the Women in Government leadership and networking group and had been introduced to the field of training and development. She discovered she really liked it, and once she received a promotion back onto the Outbound Enforcement team, she entered a Seton Hall University master's program in training and development targeted to federal law enforcement officers. "It was a different type of educational environment," Lisa Marie recalls. "K9 units would bring their dogs to class." In addition to the dogs, there was another interesting participant in one of Lisa Marie's classes—her future husband. "We dated for a long time without talking about marriage. After all, we were both in federal law enforcement and were never in the same state. It just wouldn't work."

Lisa Marie was briefly transferred to airport security before pleading her case for a position at the Training Center within the Department of Homeland Security. "There I developed the curriculum and taught future DHS leaders," she says. "It was a dream job, and there was talk that they'd make me the assistant commissioner. But by then, my boyfriend and I had decided to get married, and we thought a lot about what marriage actually meant. We realized that we couldn't both be in federal law enforcement and reside in the same place long-term. The career simply doesn't allow it."

Lisa Marie decided to leave federal law enforcement to start her own leadership training business, and instantly went from six figures to no figures. "People thought I was crazy, but I looked at it as a way to be committed to my relationship and actually help more people than I could in government," she says. "But it was a hard adjustment. In addition to the drastic income drop, I had no idea where to get clients, and I'd gone from being someone important to being anonymous. There was so much I didn't know about having my own company."

As a result of time and networking, Lisa Marie's leadership development business, Upside Thinking, Inc. (www.upsidethinking.com), has steadily gained ground. The company's mission is to teach professionals to develop a clear leadership vision, increase their sphere of influence, and achieve long-term growth and steady profits. "I spend my days delivering seminars, mostly on how to turn contacts into contracts," she says. "I meditate every morning, read something every day that helps my professional development, and evaluate every day at its end to assess what I should do differently."

Lisa Marie recommends that individuals with families consider their priorities to be 1) self, 2) family, and 3) work. "You have to identify exactly what your family's needs are, and how your career can address them," she advises. "For example, if it's time you need, sometimes you can get that without changing fields. There are jobs in most industries that don't require you to be on call 24/7. Be prepared, though, that the choices you have to make may be difficult. No one can have it all."

Today, Lisa Marie and her husband have a comfortable life in Coral Gables, Florida. Lisa Marie serves on several committees and boards including her local chamber of commerce and a local nonprofit that provides emergency relief services to the community. She recently received a Woman of Excellence Award from the National Association of Female Executives and a Woman of the Year Award from the For You Network. On her success, Lisa Marie has this to say: "I just keep on learning, and I'm really lucky to have an amazing team of mentors."

John
From International Researcher to Education Salesperson to Instructional Designer

Always intrigued by international relations, John followed up his education at the University of Notre Dame with a Ph.D. program in political science at Ohio State. After so many years of school, he was eager to go right to work for the Midwest Universities Consortium for International Activities (MUCIA). "At MUCIA, my main responsibilities were project management and grant proposal writing and research for large international projects funded by the World Bank, the Asian Development Bank, and the Inter-American Development Bank," John explains. "Even while I was getting my Ph.D., I knew that I did not want to work at a university as a professor. Instead I wanted a business job with an international focus." John spent a number of years focusing on international education and then technology education. His assignments required a great deal of travel, which John enjoyed enormously. He racked up experience in international business, negotiation, and entrepreneurship.

Meanwhile, John got married and he and his wife had three boys, each born two years apart. "After a while, international travel for ten days to two weeks at a time was no longer attractive," he says. "I did not like spending so much time away from my children and missing the important milestones in their lives." John switched to a national sales job in education technology and was soon on a fast track to promotion in a Denver-based company. But his expanding role forced him to spend every other week across the country, and when he missed his oldest son's birthday, John opted for another sales job closer to home in Columbus, Ohio.

For the next few years, John drifted from job to job, always in pursuit of the right balance of family and work—a difficult proposition in sales. Because his salary continued to increase, it was always too easy to stay in sales even as the career did not meet his family's needs or his professional aspirations. John realized he had a special gift for e-learning, but as he searched for jobs in instructional design that carried a compensation similar to that of his current sales job, it became clear that he would need to take a pay cut. "In order to make the transition, I prepared to take on extra work consulting and teaching online to supplement my income," he tells us.

In applying for the position of e-learning specialist with Micro Electronics, Inc. in Columbus, John was able to leverage his intimate knowledge and understanding of sales. Now designing interactive training courses and simulations for sales forces and their management, John is an 8 A.M.–5 P.M. employee who never travels or works weekends. "My career fits perfectly with my family obligations and I love being home every night with my wife and kids. I have not missed one soccer game, swim meet, or choral concert since I started this job," he says. And it's not just his family that's benefiting. John has realized how professionally satisfied and fulfilled he is working in instructional design. In just over a year, he has changed the way his company provides training and was put in charge of a major initiative that has him reporting directly to the vice president of human resources.

John's journey taught him that it's possible to shape a career that maintains your income but also aligns well with one's life goals. "It took a big leap of faith to suffer a twenty-five percent pay cut and become an entry-level instructional designer even though I had ten years of work experience. There was a lot of fear," John admits. "Luckily, I was able to find a position that required a background in sales. Not only am I creating content for our sales forces, but I have also given a number of internal presentations to our CEO and the executive staff. Years of sales presentations to C-level prospects certainly helped in this regard."

John feels that he brings a level of fun and creativity to his work that was missing before. And more important, he believes that he is a success on the job and at home. "My advice to other people who are looking to change careers to focus more on their family is to simply take the risk. If you find yourself away from your family on a regular basis and it hurts your heart, then you must find a career that permits you to be more involved," he says. "Review your inventory of skills from your past jobs and take a close look at what you want to do. Often, there are new careers or ways to make a career change in which you can use your past experience to become a valuable resource in your new position."

☞ Self-Reflection: Is Family Your Motivation?
- Are you so stressed out by your job that you have minimal energy to devote to your family?
- Does it pain you that your children spend long hours in day care?

- Do you and your spouse currently live in separate locations because of your jobs?
- Do you have an elderly relative who relies on you for care and support you feel you don't have time to give?
- Would you like to marry your significant other, but hesitate because you feel that your job already demands everything you have?
- Do you want to be the kind of parent who is hands-on, but can't be because of your work responsibilities?
- Do you feel like you are missing your children grow up?
- Does your spouse complain that your work is ruining your marriage?
- Does your high salary no longer provide satisfaction because you aren't around to share in its rewards?
- Is there a time every day when you find yourself feeling torn and guilty?

👍 If you answered "Yes" to two or more of these questions, you may be inspired to make a career transition in order to better address the needs of your family. Read on for some guidance on how to make it happen.

☞ Putting the Change to Work

Consider the family's financial makeup: Before you change your job situation, you need to determine if it's possible financially. In her article "7 Financial Steps Every Working Mom Needs to Know," Galia Gichon of Down-to-Earth Finance suggests taking a financial snapshot to get a better handle on your money responsibilities. It can be as simple as asking yourself the following questions:

- How much do you *owe*? Include mortgage, credit cards, student loans, personal loans, and home equity loans.
- How much do you *own*? Include all investments, bank accounts, retirement plans, and home equity.
- How much do you *spend*? This should be one number for your monthly spending. Be sure to include all those extra little expenses that wreak havoc on budgets.

• How much do you *earn?* What is your total income after taxes for the year, the month, and year-to-date?

Talk over these answers with your significant other or spouse (if you have one) to determine if your family could weather a decrease in income as you switch to a more flexible work schedule or pursue an alternative career path. Keep in mind that in addition to covering monthly expenses, you must still add to your savings. You should be contributing at least 3 percent of your income to your retirement plan, and if you don't have a 401(k) plan at work, establish an IRA. Maximizing up to the $5000 annual contribution limit by contributing $416 a month is a good idea as Social Security becomes shakier and shakier. If you're a parent, you should also make sure you are funding college education plans and life insurance coverage. Plans like the 529 allow your money to grow tax-deferred and ensure that it is free of taxes when it is withdrawn to attend an accredited university. As for life insurance, you should have adequate coverage until your youngest child is eighteen years old. Visit websites such as www.kiplinger.com to calculate your best options.

Cultivate a dual-centric point of view: Your mind-set is very important in how satisfied you are with your life over the long term. *Dual-centric* is a concept coined by Ellen Galinsky at the Families and Work Institute, and essentially it means that you place the same priority on your life on and off the job. Galinsky's study found that dual-centric individuals feel more successful at work despite putting in an average of five hours less per week. They are objectively less stressed out, and have an easier time managing the conflicting responsibilities associated with family and work. Strategies that work for dual-centric people include being clear about what's important to them, setting strict boundaries between the time they are working and not working, focusing on the immediate situation and being emotionally present when one is physically present, and taking time to rest, recover, and pursue interests outside of work.

Network with other caregivers: For working caregivers, developing friendships is often a low priority. This is understandable, for after all, any free time is usually spent struggling to keep up with errands and chores. Nevertheless, talking to other people in your position can give you valuable insights, especially when it comes to managing your career. How can you do this with minimal time and effort? Well, first of all, look for any opportunity to strike up conversations. Introduce yourself to the person standing behind you at the supermarket, or the father waiting to pick up his child at day care. Find outlets for communicating easily with other caregivers, including local area email lists and online message boards—and use them. If you can swing it, make a pact to spend an hour a week attending an event that interests you, and chat with the other attendees about their families. Find out what they do for a living, and probe them for strategies they use to balance responsibilities at work and home.

Take advantage of flextime and telework policies: In order to encourage better work/life balance, and as a response to technology that allows workers 24/7 accessibility, many organizations are implementing flextime and teleworking policies. Flextime arrangements might include part-time or compressed schedules (for example, the employee works forty hours from Monday to Thursday and takes Friday off) and job sharing, in which a full-time position is split between two people. Teleworking or telecommuting means that for at least part of the business week, an employee works from a remote location—often the home. Talk with HR and/or read your orientation materials to understand how your organization's flextime procedure works. Note that even if the company doesn't have an official policy in place, if there are other people in your department who are already working flexible schedules, it shouldn't be unreasonable for you to hop on the bandwagon—provided you can honestly say you have the self-discipline to work productively without supervision.

In making an argument for flextime, always put the company first. Your boss does not want to hear that working from home will allow you to meet your daughter's school bus. Instead, tell him that you plan to get more work done in less time due to the minimization of distractions and not having to commute. Ask for a trial of the new arrangement, and prove the cost savings by working much more efficiently at home than you do during your in-office days.

Next, put together a cohesive written proposal that details how the arrangement will work, how you will complete your assignments, how you will handle unforeseen circumstances or emergencies, and any changes in compensation and/or benefits that will result.

Once you get started, make sure that you are always accessible via email and cellphone during the business day, and report project status often so it's easy for your boss to keep tabs on you. Telework expert Gil Gordon offers these additional tips in his Work & Family Connection's e-course, Making Telecommuting Successful:

- Request weekly feedback from your supervisor on how the telecommuting arrangement is working.
- Ask for a volunteer office buddy to take responsibility for emailing you office news weekly, in return for a monthly invitation to lunch.
- Show up if necessary. People won't always be able to work around your schedule, so you may have to come in on some days you ordinarily work from home.
- If there's a meeting planned at which your work will be discussed, be sure you're invited. Volunteer to make presentations or write reports that make your deliverables more visible.
- Pay attention to perceptions. Some telecommuters notice relationships cooling with no warning, perhaps the result of a perceived slight or jealousy on the part of someone who wants to telecommute.

Look at work-from-home possibilities: Work-from-home scams abound on the Internet, so you must proceed carefully here. In her "Take Control of Your Life" series for *Good Morning America*, home work expert Tory Johnson profiles two reputable career paths that you can manage from your home. The first is home-based customer service agent. Because many large companies are cutting back on staff positions to save on salary and benefits and one of the first departments they outsource is customer service, Johnson expects that at least twenty thousand new agents will be recruited this year. Some of the better-known organizations include LiveOps (www.live

ops.com), which hires home-based salespeople and licensed insurance agents for both health and life, and Arise (www.arise.com), which recruits agents with specialized language skills.

The second option is direct seller, a career that has recently expanded beyond the typical "Avon Lady." According to the Direct Selling Association, more than 14 million Americans make a living as direct sellers, meaning they sell products or services person-to-person, outside a traditional retail location. Sellers usually have their own pages on the company's website where they can take and process orders, and allow customers to reorder online. Each time you make a sale, you earn a commission, and if you recruit people to become sellers, you'll make a small commission on their sales, too. How do you decide what to sell? Johnson recommends that you pick a product line that you are passionate about. If you can't see yourself using the products or giving the products as gifts, stay away. The Direct Selling Association (www .dsa.org) offers a list of two hundred companies in a wide variety of categories, although you should check out all prospective organizations with the Better Business Bureau to ensure they're on the up-and-up. Keep in mind that while the direct seller role is ideal for parents who care for children, it is mostly suitable for supplemental income. The median earnings in direct sales is $2,500 annually, which means 50 percent of the people in the field make more and half make less.

I'm also a fan of the twenty-first-century career of the virtual assistant (VA). I became acquainted with this job last year when I saw a segment about Karen Reddick on the *Today* show. Karen is a VA who helps run small businesses like Holland Travel in St. Louis from her home office in Colorado. Karen, the owner of V-and-E Services, is a former executive assistant and originally conceived the idea for her business after the terrorist attacks of September 11, 2001. Starting the new career was her way to put family first and be home for her teenage daughter. Karen helps clients using the latest technology to deliver creative administrative support and technical business services to busy professionals. She charges forty-five dollars an hour, and projects and personal schedules are often handled by email and instant messaging. I love the VA position because everyone involved wins. It provides business owners who might not have the cash to hire a full-time, salaried employee the ability to focus on running their operations without spending precious time and resources on administrative concerns. Plus, it allows people like Karen to do their jobs effectively, make good money, and achieve the ultimate work/life balance.

Consider traditional careers with an established second tier: According to Mary Ann Mason and Eve Mason Ekman, in their book, *Mothers on the Fast Track,* roughly half of highly educated women who begin a fast-track job will stay the course, but a substantial number, mostly mothers, will drop out or drop down to a less demanding track known as the second tier. The second tier typically has lower status, pays less, has fewer benefits and perks, and has little to no chance of major advancement. As the twenty-first century progresses, the second tier is emerging in professions such as law, medicine, and corporate management. In medicine, for example, dermatology, anesthesiology, radiology, and emergency room medicine tend to offer more reasonable hours. Second-tier options open to caregivers with law degrees include nonequity partner in a large law firm, and counselor positions in corporations, government, and nonprofit organizations. There's a second tier in academia, too—in fact, the fastest-growing segment of employees in academia is part-time and adjunct faculty. These individuals are not on a tenure track and, while they don't have the status and security of full professors, they enjoy much greater flexibility and the ability to take assignments selectively. In the years to come, Mason and Ekman hope that educated caregivers who have settled in the second tier will have an easier time reentering the top tier if they choose.

Research caregiver-friendly options: Caroline Wilbert, career and money editor for one of my content partners, DivineCaroline, suggests several jobs that are well suited for moms and others with caregiving duties. Among them are writing, teaching, by-appointment jobs, and health-care jobs. From my own research on dream jobs, I've assembled information on some of the most popular career paths in each of these categories:

- **Writing (*sample job: freelancer*):** Freelance writers develop content and articles for a variety of corporate and media outlets. They are skilled at writing, of course, but they also have excellent time management and organizational skills as well as stellar business sense. Michelle Goodman, author of *My So-Called Freelance Life*, recommends picking the brains of seasoned freelancers to get their best tips for working solo. Look at the websites, read their books and blogs, and ask questions not just about their craft, but also about how they approach specific entrepreneurial problems. Do what you can to develop ongoing relationships with these folks, because many writers get a majority of their referrals from other freelancers who are too busy to take on a project. Finally, says Goodman, make sure your computer and other equipment are up to par, and that you have a good accountant to help you out with bookkeeping and tax issues.

- **Teaching (*sample job: elementary school teacher*):** Elementary school teachers typically instruct one class of around twenty children in several subjects, including reading, writing, math, science, and social studies. Most teachers work a ten-month school year with a two-month vacation during the summer, but in some areas with a year-round schedule, the teachers work eight weeks in a row with a one-week vacation and a five-week midwinter break. According to the Bureau of Labor Statistics' *Occupational Outlook Handbook*, all states require teachers to have a bachelor's degree and to have completed an approved teacher-training program. If you're interested in transitioning to a teaching career, check out the American Federation of Teachers (www.aft.org) and the National Education Association (www.nea.org) websites. You may find that your state offers accelerated licensure due to a shortage of qualified teachers.

- **By-appointment jobs (*Sample job: life coach*):** By-appointment jobs are made up of individual engagements that caregivers can set to their liking. One such up-and-coming job is a life coach. Life coaches provide an environment to help people produce fulfilling results in their personal and professional lives, and are trained to listen, observe, and customize their approach to individual client needs. The process typically begins with a short interview so that the coach can assess the person's current challenges, priorities, and desired results. Subsequent sessions may last about sixty minutes, and between scheduled meeting times, the coach may ask the client to complete specific exercises or read materials that support behavior change and goal achievement. In order to become a life coach, you must complete a program accredited by the International Coach Federation (www.coachfederation.org). In addition to teaching necessary competencies such as establishing trust and managing progress, the program will instruct you on building your practice and persuading others of the value of your services.

- **Health-care (*sample job: physical therapist*):** The health-care sector continues to have one of the strongest growth rates in the nation, and in fact the need for qualified professionals has now surpassed the number of available workers. The demand for physical therapists, who plan and participate in rehabilitative programs to improve mobility, relieve pain, increase strength, and decrease or prevent deformity of patients suffering from disease or injury, is especially high right now. The Bureau of Labor Statistics' *Occupational Outlook Handbook* claims that nearly six out of ten physical therapists work in hospitals or in solely or jointly managed PT offices, and the others are employed with home health-care services, nursing care facilities, outpatient care centers, and adult day-care programs. Approximately 25 percent of American physical therapists currently work part-time. Gaining entry to the profession requires an accredited physical therapist educational program that takes a few years to complete and includes coursework in biology, chemistry, neuroanatomy, and human growth and development. Besides getting classroom and laboratory instruction, students receive supervised clinical experience so that they are prepared to practice immediately upon graduation.

☞ **Exercise: Assessing Your Family's Needs**

- Write down the three most critical things your family needs from you right now.

- Do you feel that your current job allows you to provide those things as effectively as you would like? Why or why not?

- Talk to your family about your work. Write down key learnings from these conversations.

- In an ideal work scenario, what would be your schedule?

- Brainstorm three ways to adapt your current career to your ideal schedule. If it's not possible, write down three new careers to research that you think would help you achieve better work/life balance.

- Inviting your spouse or significant other to contribute, make a list of the pros and cons of changing to a more family-friendly work situation.

☞ **Resource Toolkit**

Websites

BusinessWeek Working Parents blog: www.businessweek
.com/careers/workingparents/blog

Eldercare.gov: www.eldercare.gov

Executive Moms: www.executivemoms.com

Families and Work Institute: www.familiesandwork.org

Jobs and Moms Career Center: www.jobsandmoms.com

Options for Working Families: www.optionsforfamilies.org

Telecommuting 360: www.telecommuting360.com

Work It, Mom! online community: www.workitmom.com

Books

*The Milk Memos: How Real Moms Learned to Mix Business with Babies—
and How You Can, Too* (Cate Colburn-Smith and Andrea Serrette)

Will Work from Home—Earn the Cash Without the Commute (Tory Johnson
and Robyn Freedman Spizman)

CEO of Me: Creating a Life That Works in the Flexible Job Age (Ellen Ernst
Kossek and Brenda A. Lautsch)

Mothers on the Fast Track (Mary Ann Mason and Eve Mason Ekman)

*Why Work Sucks and How to Fix It: No Schedules, No Meetings, No Joke—
the Simple Change That Can Make Your Job Terrific* (Cali Ressler and
Jody Thompson)

*101 Businesses You Can Start with Less Than One Thousand Dollars: For
Stay-at-Home Moms & Dads* (Heather Shepard)

*The Creative Family: How to Encourage Imagination and Nurture Family
Connections* (Amanda Blake Soule)

*Mommy Wars: Stay-at-Home and Career Moms Face Off on Their Choices,
Their Lives, Their Families* (Leslie Morgan Steiner)

Independence

Never sing in chorus if you want to be heard.
—Jules Archibald, journalist

When I asked people I knew why they wanted to change careers, the desire for independent employment was the number-one reason I heard. The idea of working for yourself may sound like a dream that's out of reach, but in fact, the number of small businesses in the United States is growing exponentially. Recent statistics from the U.S. Small Business Administration (SBA) indicated that small firms represented 99.7 percent of all employers and were responsible for more than 45 percent of total private payroll in the United States. Small businesses make up 97 percent of all identified exporters and have generated 60 to 80 percent of net new jobs annually over the last decade. Judging from these incredible numbers, it appears that the American dream is alive and well despite the much-maligned economy.

While opportunities abound, most would agree that launching one's own business—be it a freelance operation, retail enterprise, or online venture—is a tall order. According to the SBA, two-thirds of new businesses survive at least two years, but only 44 percent survive four years. Accomplished entrepreneurs, some of whom you'll meet in this chapter, are born risk takers who are able to put aside their fear of the unknown. They define a vision, and then, using their creativity and talent for innovation, create a flesh-and-blood business in spite of the time, money, and personal sacrifice that may be required up front.

If you want to work for yourself, the motivation fueled by disliking your boss won't be enough. You'll have to think hard about an unmet marketplace need you can address via a new product or service, and learn how to uncover and employ the right mix of resources to further your cause. As you undertake the many tasks associated with getting a new business off the ground, such as brainstorming the idea that's the perfect fit for you, drafting a business plan, securing financing, and marketing, you'll be well served by daily doses of optimism, enthusiasm, and stamina. You'll have to put in a few stressful years, but hopefully you'll be rewarded with a thriving enterprise that not only pays the bills, but also allows freedom like no other type of job.

While reading the stories and advice, and completing the exercises offered in this chapter, I encourage you to do some soul-searching to determine if independent employment is right for you. For example, back in 2004 I was so fed up with corporate bureaucracy that I was dead set on forming my own communications consultancy. But once I had my own business, I quickly realized that I missed the daily social interaction of working in a large corporation and the paycheck that reliably arrived every two weeks. These considerations, however, didn't even register with some of my entrepreneur-minded friends. After a certain amount of planning and investment, they left Corporate America and never looked back.

In the event that you do decide that entrepreneurship is the best means for executing your career change, I hope that you'll leave this section with inspiration from people who have done it successfully, as well as some of the fundamentals that will help you get started today.

Kami
From Naval Officer to Energy Coordinator to Inventor

As a child, ever since one of her mom's friends gave her a book for young business owners, Kami nourished entrepreneurial dreams. Her parents, who had always worked for someone else, were conservative at heart and wanted Kami to pursue a more traditional career path. The family didn't have a lot of money, but Kami's mother didn't want Kami and her brother to miss out on college, so when the time came, she suggested the full-scholarship military academies. Kami's brother chose the U.S. Air Force Academy, while Kami headed to the U.S.

Merchant Marine Academy in Kings Point, New York. Being from Madison, Wisconsin, Kami had never seen a ship before arriving on campus, but by the time she received her degree in marine transportation, she could navigate one from point A to point B and discharge cargo without colliding with another vessel or running aground.

Kami's first job out of school was a rigorous one. She worked on the docks in Elizabeth, New Jersey—planning, coordinating, and supervising longshoremen in the loading and offloading of the ships that came into the terminal. Shortly thereafter, Kami transitioned into sales. "I sold container space on the ships," she explains. "In this role, I learned the business side of importing and exporting. My favorite part was talking to entrepreneurs and finding out how they started their businesses. It was then that I knew that I eventually wanted to import my own product. I just wasn't sure what it would be yet."

Kami was on navy reserve duty when the Iraq War began. "They needed Third Mate officers, so I volunteered," Kami says. "For the next three years, I served on ships as an officer. I delivered military cargo to Kuwait and worked on bulk ships that delivered different types of grain to Djibouti, Tanzania, Mombasa, Jordan, Bangladesh, Pakistan, and Sudan." Then she got engaged and wanted to spend more time at home with her new fiancé, so Kami decided it was time for a shoreside job. She took a position with a Norwegian energy company called StatoilHydro, operating the ships that delivered liquefied natural gas to the United States.

Kami still yearned to start her own business, but she wasn't sure where to begin. For one thing, her mother's critical attitude undermined her confidence. "Anytime I expressed what I really wanted to do, Mom discouraged it because of the wonderful benefits that my current company offered," she says. But one day while on vacation, an idea for a new product popped into Kami's head. "It was a cushion, placed on a chaise longue, with openings for the face and knees when lying on one's stomach. It was something I would have loved to ease the discomfort in my neck and back while sunning myself, and I thought others might feel the same way."

Kami launched her research as soon as she stepped off the plane. "I mostly used the Internet and joined a women's networking group," she says. "When I wasn't able to figure something out on my own, I tapped the network for advice, referrals, and assistance." Kami patented her idea, found a foam manufacturer to make the basic cutouts, and, after a shopping trip to Jo-Ann Fabrics, created an initial design with an old sewing machine she had in her attic.

Her next step, and the one that proved the most difficult, was finding a manufacturer who could make a functional and aesthetically pleasing prototype. After what seemed like hundreds of emails, Kami finally located someone suitable. The photos of her prototype stimulated interest from a wide variety of sources, from interior decorators to spas. "Once I knew there was a market for the product I was now calling the 'Spa Cushion,' I set up the warehousing, shipping, merchant account, and website. I used my salary from my job at the energy company, and also took advantage of their FedEx, fax, scanner, copier, and phone."

Kami entered the Spa Cushion (www.spacushion.com) in several competitions, and was awarded the prize for "Best Invention" by Orca Communications. This was the impetus to start generating income, and as soon as she paid off her expenses, Kami left her job at the energy company. Today, the thirty-six-year-old presides over a thriving business. "I am on email and the Internet most of the day," she says. "Right now, the Spa Cushion is offered exclusively online, so I'm prospecting—making calls to large companies and hotel chains. I do work on the road from my laptop or PDA, and I don't have to answer to anyone except my family."

Many people want to work independently, and nearly as many think they have a great idea for a new product. How did Kami pull it off? "I don't take no for an answer," she says. "I'm very persistent when I get an idea. Just ask my husband! I think outside of the box to get something accomplished in an alternative way. I'm also an honest businesswoman. Suppliers want to know that if you are sending them partial payment for a shipment, they can expect the rest upon receipt of the cargo. And I think it helps that I'm not afraid of change. I've lived in many different places and worked at many different jobs, and that's a benefit."

Like other accomplished entrepreneurs, Kami believes that an understanding of how business works is essential. "I had a basic understanding of importing from my transportation field jobs, and through research I learned how to have the product made and shipped." She also cites persistence as a virtue that prospective inventors can't live without. "If you believe in your idea, you must have the confidence and ability to stick with it even when the future looks slow and bleak," she advises. "Covet and remember the positive endorsements, and just throw out the rejections. And don't forget to share the good news with the people close to you so that they can support you through the tough times."

Ricardo
From Clarinetist to Tour Director to Food Producer

Ricardo's career as a world-class clarinetist began when his two best friends joined the band at his school in Buenos Aires, and Ricardo was left alone at the lunch table. "I wanted to play the trumpet because that was what boys played, and it was loud," he says. "But my father did not want to buy a trumpet because he said I would lose interest, and told me that if I wanted to be in the band I could play my sister's clarinet."

It didn't take long for Ricardo and the band conductor to notice that he was learning far more quickly than anyone else. He began taking private clarinet lessons, and after high school, enrolled at the National Music Conservatory in Buenos Aires. At the same time, Ricardo's father, a civil engineer with his own practice, begged Ricardo to come work with him. "I hated the idea of doing this type of work, but hated even more the thought of alienating my father and seeing him even less because my parents were divorced," says Ricardo. "We agreed that I'd go to the College of Engineering if my father supported me financially so that I could pursue my music, too."

While Ricardo was in school, he worked with his father part-time and switched his concentration to land surveying, but at graduation he decided to join the Municipal Band in Moreno. His father reluctantly accepted his choice, but did not hesitate to tell Ricardo that it was a bad one. "I now realize that part of the reason I became a clarinetist was that my father didn't want me to," Ricardo admits. He soon found, however, that the life of a young musician was hardly easy. As a public employee with the Municipal Band, Ricardo felt like a bureaucrat doing something mediocre at the taxpayers' expense. "I even entertained the idea that it was immoral to play classical music in front of poor people who would have picked a bag of rice over a Schubert march." After just a few months with the Municipal Band, a new mayor dissolved the band and Ricardo was out of work.

He auditioned repeatedly for the National Radio Youth Orchestra in Buenos Aires, and finally got in at the age of twenty. There he played the best music of his life, but was disheartened by the orchestra's alliances, rivalries, backstabbing, and cutthroat competition. After he was suspended for missing a dress rehearsal, Ricardo resigned. "Everyone thought I was crazy," he says. "But the truth is that I had set a goal, and once I had accomplished it, it lost its appeal and I was ready to move on."

Ricardo's immense talent kept him constantly employed, though, and before long he was a member of the most prominent band in Argentina and making enough money to relocate to the United States. He continued his clarinet studies at the Mannes College of Music in New York City and won a position with the prestigious New York Symphony, an orchestra Ricardo had admired for years. "I rehearsed and practiced, practiced and rehearsed," he says. "The schedule was difficult, but the music was glorious and the musicians played magnificently." But a lifetime career as a respected performance musician was not to be. Still in his twenties, Ricardo was diagnosed with focal dystonia, a neurological condition that causes muscular contractions. "It's possible that this was a psychosomatic manifestation of an inner desire to quit music," muses Ricardo. "My father had embraced my music career, and now that I had his blessing, I lost interest in the clarinet."

Ricardo decided to turn his side gig as a Manhattan tour director into a full-time job. He began training to lead ten-day tours for fifty or more passengers in the northeastern United States and eastern Canada. The difference between being a musician and a tour director was startling. The life of a musician is often solitary, whereas tour directors are never alone and are constantly interacting with others. What was most difficult for Ricardo, though, was overcoming his stammering. "I had done speech therapy back in Argentina, but I still stuttered. Being a tour director allowed me to practice my speaking skills and overcome the disability," he says proudly.

Ricardo was earning a solid income as a tour guide based in New York when an insight hit him as he rode the number 7 subway train to Times Square. "I saw two people eating a burger and slice of pizza, and they were making a mess. I wondered why they were not eating empanadas—handheld baked pies—which are the perfect meal-on-the-go," he explains. "And I immediately got an idea: Why not introduce baked empanadas to the American market?" The more Ricardo thought about it, the more sense it made. He liked the idea of working independently and being charged with his own destiny. His research convinced him that he had come across something with potential.

Ricardo had always liked to cook, but he had no experience with food production or business. He enrolled in an MBA program at the Zicklin School of Business at Baruch College in Brooklyn. There he was encouraged to analyze his idea from every angle—from marketing and finance to organizational behavior and operations. The business plan for Rico M. Panada, LLC (www.ricompanada.com) won Baruch's Entrepreneurship Competition, and the company was officially launched in 2004.

Never before has Ricardo been so busy. He wakes at 5 A.M., getting to his plant in the Bronx at around 6 A.M. During the packed twelve-hour day, Ricardo performs inspections, records findings for the regulatory agencies, supervises employees, and helps with production and packing. "As a business owner, if I decide to take the day off, I can do it. I don't have to ask for permission. That is invaluable to the libertarian inside me," says Ricardo. "And when I'm at Whole Foods buying my groceries and I see the person in front of me with a box of my empanadas in her basket, I feel a profound spiritual satisfaction."

Ricardo is one of the rare few who have flourished in three very different careers. His formula involves open-mindedness, curiosity, and the ability to adapt quickly. "Moving from one country to another, I've learned to master others' ways and incorporate them."

He doesn't regret for a moment what has turned into a winding path. "Studying land surveying provided a strong mathematical foundation that is useful now that I run a business, while being a clarinetist instilled self-discipline that I have applied ever since. Finally, being a tour director taught me patience and an understanding of human nature. That work proved to me that stereotypes are just a product of the imagination, and that to sell anything effectively you have to engage in a conversation with the customer, identify his needs, and tailor the offering so that it satisfies those needs." Spoken like a true entrepreneur!

Liene
From Accountant to Wedding Planner

As a young twenty-something, Liene was always the one her friends asked to help them plan their weddings. Even though she had gone to Arizona State University for psychology, Liene had extensive event experience. Between high school and college, she had taken a few years off to work at a nonprofit and had organized many a fundraiser in her time. She far preferred weddings, though. "All events are interesting in that you get to see a lot of moving parts finally come together, but I love helping people celebrate the significant moments in their lives, and weddings are a wonderful blend of cultures, traditions, and families," Liene explains.

When Liene graduated from college, she became not an event planner or even a counselor, but an accountant at telecommunications software firm Inter-Tel. "No one's beating down your door to give you a job in psychology unless you have a graduate degree, and I needed to pay my bills," she says. "I'd worked at a bank during college, so I had the right experience for a job in accounting." Liene quickly realized, however, that cubicle life was not for her. "I sat there all day crunching numbers, talking to the same people over and over, but you do what you have to do."

One evening, Liene attended an awards ceremony for a colleague who had been with the company twenty-eight years. "The moment was seared in my brain. I knew that wasn't where I wanted to be," she says. Shortly afterward, she began suffering from sporadic paralysis and her doctors thought she had multiple sclerosis. "I was sick for about two and a half years, and I had to take a leave of absence." Fortunately, Liene recovered and was able to work at a series of jobs, including one as a designer for a friend's wedding invitation shop. As she learned more and more about how the wedding industry operated, Liene gradually came to believe that she would be better off starting her own event planning business. "I wanted the opportunity to work with a variety of people, and to create a schedule that would allow for my future life as a wife and mother," she says. "I didn't want to be a slave to my job. I would rather be the person who's able to go to dance recitals on Saturday mornings."

In her mid-twenties, Liene launched Blue Orchid Designs (www .blueorchidweddings.com) in Scottsdale, Arizona. The business, which orchestrates luxury weddings from top to bottom, took a year to become profitable. During this period, Liene supported herself with her savings and a very lean marketing budget that consisted only of a blog. "When you don't have a lot of start-up capital, you are forced to get creative," she says. "I don't have a business degree, and I think in many ways my naïveté was useful. I would just call up vendors and other planners and ask them to lunch because I didn't even think about the fact that they might perceive me as competition. I was genuinely interested in getting to know them, and building those relationships helped me."

Liene found that her experience with psychology and accounting came in handy as well. "I was able to recognize that sometimes a stressed-out bride or mother just needs someone to listen, not a prescription for Xanax," she says. "Also, most small business owners use Quicken and never quite get the accounting side up to par, but because I worked at Inter-Tel, I was equipped to run my accounts receivable and payable functions as efficiently as a major corporation."

Liene's day consists of working from a home office, exchanging multitudes of emails with couples who are organizing destination weddings, visiting vendors with clients, and figuring out the math of how many bodies and tables will fit into an event space. Her goal in planning is to bring a couple's story out in the details and to provide an experience that's fun and not necessarily mired in tradition. Working with Blue Orchid Designs, Liene has overcome her natural shyness and realized that she's not as sensitive as she thought. "I don't get upset if someone decides to go with a different planner," she says. She has also learned that she's a goal setter—and achiever. "I wanted to bring on a few associate consultants so that I didn't have to do everything myself, and so I could reap the benefits of multiple income streams. I thought it would take much longer, but I've already been able to do it. Sometimes, I'm more surprised than anyone."

Liene's most important insight in becoming an entrepreneur, though, is that it's the normal, everyday people who make things happen. "I used to think that CEOs were these mythical creatures, and that it wasn't possible to reach their level," she says. "Even in the wedding planning world, I believed Martha Stewart set the trends. But then it occurred to me that I could shape the industry, too. If I say something is a trend and take pictures of it, then it's a trend."

Liene advises other prospective business owners to launch as soon as they are able. "If you wait until everything is in order, it will never happen. Ask your spouse or family to help you out, be prepared to pinch pennies for a while, and then just go for it. It won't be perfect, but it will be yours."

Scott
From Firefighter to Automotive Manufacturer to Software Developer to Global Adventurer

Thirty-five-year-old Scott wasn't always a precision driver and professional racer, working on special vehicle projects for Jeep and Toyota and driving in off-road races. Many moons ago, he received an associate's degree in fire science. "My father, uncle, and grandfather were all firemen at one time or another, so it was an early interest for me," says Scott, who grew up in Sherman Oaks, California, competing in triathlons and going bird hunting with his dad. "I was a full-time firefighter in the air force for four years, but while it was an honorable career, it lacked the mental challenges I desired."

Scott married his high school sweetheart, Stephanie, and went back to school to earn a bachelor's of science in business management. His first job after graduation was in high-volume automotive component manufacturing. At the time, the choice made sense. Scott was inspired and excited by the opportunity to work for a start-up with a brand-new facility, and he was promised that he would advance quickly. Scott got his start managing production reporting, then moved up to materials management, and finally landed an executive position overseeing operations. Although it was at times bureaucratic, Scott's first job provided an ideal environment to master the complexities of working within a large organization.

After losing a tremendous amount of business to China in 2001, Scott's facility closed, and he declined the invitation to move to the sister facility in Rochester, New York. He instead accepted a position at Interface Management Services, a higher education consulting and software development firm based in Southern California. Initially, Scott was a project management consultant for large student information system deployments, and eventually helped launch the company's successful interface development practice. "I often worked at client sites or at home, with little office interaction," Scott says. "I learned how to operate autonomously, cultivate client relationships, and act quickly when opportunities presented themselves. One thing's for sure—my experience with two start-ups muted my fear of risk."

Scott had always wanted to have his own business, and now he had the framework to launch one. He identified a pending shift in the world of adventure travel and a gaping hole in the marketplace, and got to work developing a strategic vision, earning capital, and retaining world-class resources. It took Scott two years to fully transition to a new career as the owner of a new adventure travel organization, Expeditions West (www.expeditionswest.com). The company's mission is to provide expedition training and marketing to the automotive and outdoor industries—supporting clients who are filming movies in South America, competing in international car races in Africa, and designing all-terrain military vehicles. "In the beginning, I conducted several proof-of-concept expeditions. These resulted in sponsorship agreements and consulting contracts that allowed me to reinvest in the business," explains Scott. "During that time, I became a miser with personal expenses. I cut up all of my credit cards and eliminated all personal debt with the exception of my mortgage." Making the career shift debt free required considerable commitment, careful planning, and long hours on Scott's part. Fortunately, Expeditions West did well early on, which fueled expansion and profit. In 2007, Scott had enough capital to launch two companion businesses, *Overland Journal*, a full-color quarterly magazine, and Overland Video, a production company.

The desire to work on his own in an unpredictable and fluid setting led Scott to create a virtual office, which consists of a global cellphone, a BGAN terminal (Broadband Global Area Network satellite Internet and ISDN), and an Apple MacBook Pro. "Everything around me changes—the scenery, the languages, the temperatures, and the longitude and latitude. Each day is entirely different from the one before. I can wake up in a hundred-thousand-dollar Earth-Roamer expedition vehicle or a Bedouin tent on the Algerian border. I'll consult with Jeep or provide logistics support to the Special Forces. I might be driving a race truck in Morocco or testing the newest Land Cruiser in Arizona," he enthuses.

Scott feels blessed to have had the chance to work through the challenges of a new business. "At the end of the day, both the successes and the failures are yours, and that ownership is very real and very powerful." He continually reaches new levels of achievement because he's unfailingly optimistic, and will always take the risk even if it may result in failure. Scott calls himself a connector—a person who is effective at bringing together people and ideas for a worthy outcome. He certainly has boundless energy, sleeping just four or five hours a night!

When he's not globetrotting, Scott lives in Prescott, Arizona, with Stephanie and their Alaskan malamute, Yukon. He is the only American to win Australia's high-profile Outback Challenge race, and spends his precious free time writing, canyoneering, and mountain biking. He and Stephanie are looking forward to starting a family at the conclusion of their South American and Antarctica expeditions next year.

Every week, Scott receives an email from someone asking how they can get his job. "Essentially, I believe the biggest mistake people make with lifestyle career changes is going in with a lack of business acumen and a lack of capital," he says. "They are often passionate, but simply don't have proper knowledge of accounting, permits, marketing, sales, and budgeting." He recommends that would-be entrepreneurs draft a vision document that gets the core ideas and plans on paper. "Define the key attributes for success," he says. "Are there customers for your widget? Does a town of two thousand really need another coffee shop? Create a business plan in which you clearly define your brand and scope, and then find a mentor to audit the plan. Save or secure sufficient capital, identify resources to overcome your weaknesses, launch with a bang, and then hold on for the ride!"

Kim
From Visual Merchandiser to Mortgage Broker to Gallery Owner

Thirty-eight-year-old Kim has always been enthusiastic about art, but it wasn't until two major career changes that she was able to pursue it full-time. The first change, she says, was for family. She went into a business she didn't enjoy because her husband needed her. Her second change was for love.

At eighteen, Kim received a full academic scholarship to Monmouth University in West Long Branch, New Jersey. She started out with a major in international business, but disliked the coursework so much that she switched to fine arts halfway through her sophomore year. During her year studying abroad in London, Kim worked as a window displayer at Selfridges department store, where she arranged miniature opera house sets. The following year, she did an internship in the graphic design department of the Franklin Institute Science Museum in Philadelphia, then returned to Monmouth, where she graduated cum laude.

Kim's first job out of college was with an electronics company, Nobody Beats the Wiz, which at the time owned about twenty stores in the New York City area. "They were expanding and opening some new locations, so they were looking for a window display and store setup team," says Kim. "When they found out that I knew how to work their new vinyl sign die-cut machine, they hired me on the spot." Kim worked for the company until it declared Chapter 11 five years later. The job took its toll. "I often worked sixty to ninety hours a week and twenty-four hours straight to get a new store open by the deadline." She disliked contending with office politics in what was then a family-owned business, and she found herself having to invent new processes where none existed.

After Nobody Beats the Wiz, Kim accepted a position as a visual merchandising communications manager for Lady Foot Locker—creating floor and window displays for more than one thousand stores. Then, at the age of twenty-eight, she got married. "My new husband owned a small mortgage company and I left my job to help him out. We opened two new branches in a different state," she explains. "It was very entrepreneurial, and I didn't realize until this experience how much I enjoyed working for myself. After that first taste, I was hooked!"

However, Kim later regretted tying her career to her husband's, when they divorced. "I took about six months to meditate on the type of job that would make me happy and hold my interest over the next five, ten, twenty years. I knew that I loved the risks and rewards of own-ing my own business, and thought about types of operations in which I could turn what I did for enjoyment—appreciating art—into a career."

After coming upon the idea of purchasing an art gallery, Kim faced a difficult transition. In order to avoid getting overwhelmed, she pro-ceeded logically: bringing in professionals to help with areas where she had little experience, hiring an attorney to review her contracts and incorporate her business, and enlisting an accountant to comb the financials of the gallery before Kim took over. Two unexpected obstacles were her age and gender. As a female who looked younger than she was, people constantly underestimated her. "For example, a customer might say he wanted to speak with the owner, and would walk right past me to my gallery director, a fifty-eight-year-old man."

The biggest stressor in her new venture, though, was Kim's uncertainty about what would happen next. "It caused many sleep-less nights," she admits. "But when I was afraid of something, I just researched the heck out of it, and then it lost its power over me. Now, a few years into running the business, I have very little fear. I now understand how some people can make a fortune, lose it, and then make it again."

Kim's life as the owner of the Karin Newby Gallery (www.karin newbygallery.com) in the tourist town of Tubac, Arizona, revolves around the seasons. "During the town's busy season, I concentrate more on daily management—serving customers, accounting, selling on the floor, wining and dining artists, and even cleaning the bathroom," she says. "When things are slow, I try to work on the business rather than in the business. I reflect on what has worked with respect to artists, products, and marketing, and I come up with a plan for the following season. I determine the schedule of events, write the press releases, and design the advertising. I also travel a lot more, seeking out new artists to represent in the gallery."

It sounds like a lot of work, but Kim chose her business wisely. "My aunts own Roseman's Florist in Punxsutawney, Pennsylvania. When I was talking about starting my own company, they told me to think hard before getting into a business that would require my own labor to create the final product. As florists, they never had a holiday off and were always trying to move product that spoiled quickly." Thanks in part to this advice, Kim established herself in a business that is run on consignment and therefore has low overhead, with a product that stays valuable over time. Art emergencies are rare, and it's unusual for Kim to be stuck in the gallery after hours.

Kim recommends that independence seekers purchase an existing business, as she did. "There are business brokers that act as real estate agents. This is nice because you can see how the business is doing in its current location and get a clear picture of its financial history. If you identify a business that calls out for your improvement, then you've got a huge head start." Out in Tubac, Kim continues to challenge herself. "I would love to offer fine crafts and gift items as well, but I couldn't do it in our location, so I'm launching an online catalog called Indigo Desert Ranch in the fall." We'll wish her luck!

☞ Self-Reflection: Is Independence Your Motivation?

- Are you constantly thinking up ideas for new businesses, services, or products?

- Do you long to control your own hours so you can have a better balance between your personal and professional lives?
- Are you exhausted by the thought of the office politics in your company?
- Do you consistently get your work done without your boss looking over your shoulder?
- Do you find that you're more productive when you don't have to stay within the confines of a set schedule?
- Are you often motivated to take on new projects outside the realm of your responsibility because you see problems that need fixing?
- Would your colleagues describe you as a "jack-of-all-trades"?
- Does the idea of living paycheck to paycheck for a while excite you to some degree?
- Does having total control over your income appeal to you?
- Do you tell your friends who complain about their lives that "people have to make their own luck"?

👍 If you answered "Yes" to two or more of these questions, you may want to take measures to work for yourself. To get started, check out the advice ahead.

☞ Putting the Change to Work

Brainstorm ideas: Sitting down with a pen and paper—either by yourself or with a creative group of friends or colleagues—is a terrific way to generate a working list of potential new business ideas. Steven Gold, author of *Entrepreneur's Notebook*, advocates the following five-step brainstorming process:

- Develop a set of initial criteria by listing specific resources, expertise, limitations, and goals.
- Pick a starting point—an industry, interest, or issues. Create a list of ideas associated with that starting point, and then evaluate it according to your criteria, eliminating some ideas and focusing on others.
- Using your short list, write down as many problems associated

with each item as you can think of. Rate the problems and create a new, prioritized list.

- Generate a list of solutions.
- Based on these solutions to the problems, come up with a list of potential business opportunities.

Note that good ideas will be ones that you are passionate about and motivated by, but will not necessarily be 100 percent original. In fact, some of the most successful new businesses take an already established concept and make improvements to it, or simply target a new audience.

Write yourself a reality check: Many of us have fun business ideas that we enjoy sharing with friends over cocktails, but before you start pouring money and resources into yours, take the time to consider if the idea is truly viable. You will no doubt have eliminated some unrealistic propositions as part of the brainstorming process, but you should also perform a more in-depth cash-flow analysis (see the exercise later in the chapter) to determine the exact resources that will be required. If, for instance, you find that your idea will cost millions of dollars, will involve something illegal, or will require a level of expertise that you can't easily obtain, then you probably want to go back to the brainstorming phase.

Test your concept: The next step is to tap the market to see if customers will buy what you're selling. Speak informally to key decision makers, read industry reports and publications, run focus groups, and sweep the Internet for news about potential competitors. The bottom line, says Gold, is to confirm with some degree of certainty that your proposed new venture can deliver the goods, effectively compete for new customers, and make a profit. You will need to design your product or service in a way that sets your business apart from the competition while also keeping costs under control.

Consider freelancing or consulting: "If the thought of hunting for new work each week or month and selling yourself to prospective clients excites you, you're motivated to meet deadlines without a boss lurking down the hall, you have the business sense of a Boston Terrier, and you enjoy working by your lonesome, a freelancing or consulting career might be for you," says Michelle Goodman, author of *My So-Called Freelance Life*. How do you break in? First, decide on your service offering and put together a portfolio of work samples. If you're a writer, designer, or programmer, it's easier, but if not, it might require a bit more thought to formulate exactly what you'll bring to your customers. "Can you, for example, manage projects, advise on strategy, conduct research, or revamp processes?" says Pamela Skillings, author of *Escape from Corporate America*. "It's important to be proactive about defining what you can do and not just wait around for potential clients to tell you what they need." In addition to the tips she offers with respect to freelance writing in chapter one, Goodman suggests getting to know individuals in freelancing organizations such as the Freelancers Union (www.freelancersunion.org) and Mediabistro (www.mediabistro.com), and asking them about the going rate for your line of work, in your location, with your level of experience. While you're in the process of building a client base, you'll want to be prepared to negotiate down. And speaking of building a client base, you can start with online freelance marketplaces such as ELance.com. Also, "search for freelance or contract positions on the bigger job boards and Craig's List," adds Skillings. "Make a note of the staffing agencies that have posted attractive opportunities and contact them directly to ask about other openings."

Consider inventing a new product: Before you begin, make sure someone else hasn't thought of your idea already. Hit the Internet and look for products similar to yours in indexes such as ThomasNet (www.thomasnet.com) and Harris Infosource (www.harrisinfo.com). Also, take a look at the companies that manufacture these products to see if your offering could compete effectively with theirs. Your next step is to check out the U.S. Patent and Trademark Office's online database (www.uspto.gov) to find related patents that were recently filed. If your research proves that your idea is unique, follow the process for obtaining a patent. When this is complete, you'll need to choose how you're going to sell your product. Your options are 1) licensing—getting an established manufacturer to buy your invention and pay you a royalty on those sales, and 2) venturing—starting a business to manufacture and sell the product yourself.

Go retail: Might your career change involve owning a high-end children's clothing boutique or the Subway restaurant down the block? An early decision will involve whether to start your business from the ground up, buy an existing operation, or purchase a franchise license. Of the three options, starting from scratch is probably the most difficult, for an established business brings a built-in location, inventory, and a customer base, and a franchise license offers national name recognition and recognizable branding, predetermined costs, and a set management model. However, with existing businesses and franchises, you'll have to give up decision-making power and the freedom to shape the operation just so. For more information on franchise opportunities, check out groups such as Gaebler Ventures (www.gaebler.com), which offers thousands of franchise options in a single online directory, and *Entrepreneur*'s Franchise 500 listing for details on the top franchises and their start-up requirements.

Regardless of whether you own a new or existing business, your retail operation should have a location that is relatively secure and accessible by public transportation. In its specialty publication *How to Start a Retail Store,* the magazine *Entrepreneur* suggests positioning yourself next to noncompetitive retail businesses that have steady clients, because the overflow from these businesses will drive your walk-in traffic. Before you finalize the arrangements for your new space, obtain your business and resale licenses, a small business credit card, and insurance. If securing product inventory is on your agenda, research local and online wholesalers and manufacturers who carry the items you're interested in, and find out where and when you can attend trade shows and markets.

Employ an online-only model: EBay is only the beginning. Online businesses are increasing in popularity as they provide ways to generate revenue beyond the sale of your products or services (for example, you can sell advertising space or recommend affiliate products on your site). Here are a few tips if an online store is in your entrepreneurial future. First, pick a name for your business that's easy to spell and type into a Web browser, then create a site that's easy to navigate and search, and, if you're conducting financial transactions online, that provides simple checkout, accepts credit cards, and makes it easy to find and contact live customer service. If you don't have substantial Web design and programming expertise, your best bet is to go with a professional host such as eBay's Pro-Stores (www.prostores.com) or Yahoo! Merchant Solutions (small-business.yahoo.com/merchant). These all-in-one solutions provide a mix of site-building tools, product catalog tools, shopping-cart technology, payment processing, shipping and inventory management, accounting tools, tracking and reporting capabilities, and domain registration. Just make sure you test your site repeatedly before opening up for business, since you'll want to be certain that you can handle heavy customer traffic and all types of transactions.

Develop your business plan: No matter what type of independent business you're contemplating, putting together a comprehensive business plan will help you to clarify and research your new offering, provide a framework for growth over the first three to five years, and be an important tool in your conversations with potential partners and investors. Typical business plans include a vision statement, or your beliefs about what the business should be and what you see it becoming; a mission statement, or what your business will provide and to whom; and a situation analysis, or the current status of the market. It should also incorporate an operations section, where you'll detail how you'll run the business; a marketing section, where you'll detail how you'll let people know about your business; and a sales section, where you'll detail how you'll recruit new customers and retain existing ones. You'll conclude with a finances section that will include your budgeted costs and how your business will turn a profit.

Secure funding: Many fledgling businesses fail due to a lack of start-up capital. However, you don't have to have a trust fund or a rich relative to get money for your new venture. There are many types of grants offered to new entrepreneurs, including individual grants, business grants, and government grants. State development agencies and community banks, for instance, frequently provide financial assistance to new business owners. If you have a solid business plan and excellent negotiation skills, you can also try to interest an angel investor, or a high-net-worth individual who invests in new companies, usually at an early stage. Like institutional venture capital firms, many angel investors provide cash to young companies and take equity in return.

Seek experienced counsel: As a new entrepreneur, it's essential that you recruit a more established mentor to offer wisdom, advice, connections, and moral support. A good mentor might be in your industry, or another entrepreneur with a different type of business. Once you find someone appropriate, read his written materials and Google him to learn as much as you can about his career. Get in touch by email to start, and then outline your expectations for engagement. These should involve getting together at least once a quarter to discuss your business and to challenge your assumptions on how things should be done. You might also want to join a support group or third-party industry association so that you have the opportunity to brainstorm with your peers and compare notes on what's working and what isn't. Keep in touch by subscribing to their Listservs and newsletters. As a new inventor, for example, you can hook up with your local Chamber of Commerce or your local branch of organizations such as the Professional Inventors Alliance (www.piausa.org) or the United Inventors Association (www.uiausa.org).

Build your team: According to Jeff and Rich Sloan, the founders of StartupNation, the best way to do this is to create a superstar list. Write down the names of twelve people who have special gifts and with whom you would like to work, without limiting yourself to people who could fit a current need on your team. Look for people with potential, people with proven skills, and people who are power brokers. Hiring people with potential is less expensive and will allow for growth into a position. Hiring people with proven skills will quickly fill in areas where your business is weak. Power brokers wield a great deal of influence in your community or industry. If creating a superstar list from your existing network doesn't meet all your needs, meet viable candidates cheaply through third-party association events, competitors, or social networking sites such as Facebook and LinkedIn.

Manage the business side: The U.S. Small Business Administration (www.sba.gov) is a terrific resource for logistical information, such as how to acquire health and other types of insurance, licenses, and discounts on supplies such as business cards and services such as web programming, to help you start your new, independent career. You should also enlist the services of a good accountant and lawyer. Your accountant will be responsible for reviewing your business's books and accurately recording its financial details, preparing tax returns, and overseeing your budgeting and future projections. Your lawyer, says Gold, should help you establish your new venture as a legal entity (sole proprietorship, corporation, etc.), determine how equity is issued in your new company, create an ownership structure, outline how employees, consultants, and advisers will be integrated into the business, and prepare for future legal issues involving investment and operations. Incorporate your budget for these professionals into your cash-flow analysis, and hire those who have experience working with entrepreneurs and who have been referred by trusted colleagues and verified by client references. Once they're on board, establish a protocol for regular communication and a timeline for reaching agreed-upon goals.

Get the word out: New entrepreneurs usually don't have the budget for splashy advertising campaigns or high-priced publicists. Therefore, you'll need to get a little more creative when it comes to marketing your business. Low-cost suggestions include making alliances with related community groups or local companies, sending out a monthly email newsletter, teaching adult education classes, and speaking at nonprofit organization meetings in your industry. Build a professional website on which you feature core information about your business and promote your expertise via articles you've written or been quoted in. Make your site search-engine friendly by having domain names, page titles, and copy that are relevant to your trade, and link to similar sites with good reputations and high traffic. Finally, identify online communities where your target customers gather. Get a feel for each and then offer your educated opinion—sales-pitch free.

☞ **Exercise: Prepare a Cash-Flow Analysis for Your Independent Career**

A simple cash-flow analysis will help you ascertain how much money you will need to launch and maintain your business, how much you can put back into the business, and how much you will have left over for personal expenses and savings. In addition to following the steps below, look at online examples of cash-flow statements (at websites like www.accountingcoach.com) to fully get your arms around the concept. Note that this exercise should be completed during the business planning phase, after much thought and research has already gone into your idea.

- **Step One:** Estimate your annual gross income for your first year of operation, including start-up capital that you plan to invest. Estimate an amount for circumstances that will prevent the business from running at full potential (customer freebies, sick days, etc.), and subtract it.

- **Step Two:** Compile a list of the expenses, by category, which you will incur to operate the business. Include things like offices, equipment and supplies, inventory, utilities, salaries, insurance, legal and accounting fees, taxes, business travel, and marketing expenditures. Add these together, and place the total "expenses" number underneath the gross income figure.

- **Step Three:** Calculate the total payments you will make to the bank for loans, mortgages, or other financing. Add these together and label your final total "debt." Place the debt number beneath the expenses figure.

- **Step Four:** Subtract the total expenses and the total debt from the annual income number. This is your cash-flow analysis for the year.

- **Step Five:** Input your data into a spreadsheet program like Microsoft Access or Excel, and update it weekly once your business is in operation. Need a more complex version? Check out QuickBooks (www.quickbooks.intuit.com) or download planning forms for free at websites like www.planware.org.

☞ **Resource Toolkit**

Websites

Entrepreneur.com: www.entrepreneur.com
Freelancers Union: www.freelancersunion.org
Ladies Who Launch: www.ladieswholaunch.com
National Association for the Self-Employed: www.nase.org
National Venture Capital Association: www.nvca.org
NOLO (small business legal companion): www.nolo.com
Small Business Administration: www.sba.gov
Wall Street Journal Startup Journal: startup.wsj.com

Books

The One Minute Entrepreneur (Ken Blanchard, Don Hutson, and Ethan Willis)
My So-Called Freelance Life (Michelle Goodman)
Entrepreneur's Notebook (Steven Gold)
The Art of the Start (Guy Kawasaki)
Harvard Business Essentials: Entrepreneur's Toolkit (Richard Luecke)
Escape from Corporate America (Pamela Skillings)
Escape from Cubicle Nation (Pamela Slim)
Accidental Branding (David Vinjamuri)

Learning

Genius without education is like silver in the mine.
—**Benjamin Franklin, inventor and politician**

I've always been a person who has loved to learn. School was never a chore for me, and now I watch those educational videos my teachers used to put on for us on Friday afternoons—for fun. Many people are surprised that I haven't yet gone back for an advanced degree, and the truth is that I would love to. I'm not sure what a master's degree will buy me careerwise, but given that formal education holds a great deal of personal value for me, I see myself making some sacrifices to pursue it in the near future.

For many, a natural curiosity about the world and a desire to expand their skills and research answers to pressing questions translate into an innate need to return to the academic world. Others want to use formal education to better themselves and their career prospects. In general, this works. According to Back to College (*www.back2college .com*), a recent report from the U.S. Census Bureau indicated that the median annual income for employees with a high school diploma was just over $27K. For those with a bachelor's degree, it was $51K, and for those with a master's or doctoral degree, it was above $74K.

Going back to school in your twenties or thirties or beyond doesn't necessarily mean donning your RollerBlades to cruise through a well-manicured campus. Education of all types, including certification programs, vocational training, and distance learning, is on the rise. However, despite the varied options, taking the time out of an already packed schedule to take coursework is a challenge, and you should be sure you understand your motives and desired outcomes before embarking on the path. Your loved ones will be an important part of your decision-making process, and once you're ready to move forward, careful planning will be necessary to ensure that you get the most out of your experience.

The individuals you'll meet in this chapter returned to the classroom to fulfill a part of themselves long neglected, and found that they were able to make career changes that would radically influence the direction of their lives. If the learning bug is nipping at your heels, I hope that this section assists you in taking the right steps to investigate and enroll in the program that's best for you.

Ryan
From Wine Connoisseur to Thought Leader Promoter

Thirty-three-year-old Ryan had always intended to pursue a career in international relations. He even received a degree in it from the University of San Francisco, finishing magna cum laude. Ryan first considered law school as a next step, but after interning and taking coursework, decided it wasn't for him. Then Ryan thought he'd get a job at the U.S. Agency for International Development—until a few months before his college graduation, when the government agency experienced a hiring freeze.

Dejected, Ryan took off for Europe and held a variety of odd jobs there, including opening a restaurant in London. When he returned to the United States, a friend referred him to a high-growth company that had recently gone public. "I was hired as an associate in the investor relations department and hated every minute of it," says Ryan. "I decided quickly that I needed to find something related to what I was passionate about—culture and fine food and wine."

Ryan considers his first job with a premium winery an excellent introduction to the wine business. "I worked for a well-known family winery and was able to enjoy great success," he remembers. "I helped the winery to expand distribution, increase its profitability, and open a couple of offshoot businesses." Ryan established a wine education program for the trade and general public and spent his evenings and mornings working alongside the head winemaker to learn as much as he could about the industry.

He also slept very little, for during his twenties Ryan started his own apparel business on the side. "We were able to get some decent distribution while we mastered the ins and outs of entrepreneurship. We got out without making a ton of money, but without losing much, either." Still excited by the wine business, Ryan and his new wife moved to Chicago, the most competitive wine market in the United States, so that Ryan could work for an importer and distributor of fine wines. Directing a business unit focusing on the highest-end wines in the portfolio, Ryan was the youngest member of the senior executive team and soon established a strong reputation. But then, his company was purchased by a multibillion-dollar corporation. "During the transition, I took the time to think about the many opportunities I was being offered, and what they would mean for my future," he says. "I missed being an entrepreneur, and figured that if I could run a large business for another person, I could certainly do it for myself."

Much as he loved wine, Ryan felt that the industry lacked innovation and moved too slowly for him. His passion for learning and intellectual challenges left him with a hankering to go back to school and study entrepreneurship. Ryan was lucky to be offered a full fellowship to Babson College, which has the best entrepreneurship program in the world. "I received a great deal of support from my wife," he says. "I had to move halfway across the country to pursue this path, and there were a lot of people who thought I was nuts turning away from a flourishing career." But even once in school, Ryan went against the grain. "I went in not knowing what industry I wanted to start a business in. I was just inspired by the potential of entrepreneurship. Yet everyone wanted me to focus. I had to convince them that all industries have the same patterns and that I could apply what I was learning to a wide range of businesses."

Life at Babson was more fulfilling than Ryan could have imagined. He expanded his network and learned that entrepreneurship is tough but addictive. "It's about reaching toward your vision with limited resources, and surrounding yourself with talented people," he tells us. "I also came to the conclusion that experience is an odd concept. There are people who have been doing something for twenty years, but have been going about it poorly or wrong. You can do very well if you've only been at something for a year but have gone about it the right away all along."

Thanks in part to the contacts he made at Babson, Ryan was able to launch a Web application company upon receiving his MBA. "We operate in a few industries, including music, publishing, and marketing, and business is good. One of our businesses is Learn From My Life (www.learnfrommylife.com), a Web-enabled community that connects inspirational thought leaders and bestselling authors with a global audience interested in personal and professional growth," he says. "It offers my partner and me the opportunity to interact with the most amazing individuals on a daily basis. I'm so glad I had the guts to make a big change, because now I'm enjoying the rewards. I'm engaged every day, and unlike my old career in wine, I have no idea what my work will be like in ten or twenty years."

Though Ryan still works long hours, he has been able to infuse his life with greater balance. "I've gotten back to playing soccer regularly, something I've loved doing since I was a kid. I sneak in a few surf sessions when the ocean isn't packed with weekend warriors, I get to play with my new daughter in the mornings, and I sometimes hang out with my wife in the middle of the day. Those things don't have a price tag."

For Ryan, the desire to learn and to use his newfound knowledge to affect his world has always been a major motivator. It was inevitable that he would return to school in some capacity, and he has this advice for similarly minded people: "Understand why you want to go back to school, and figure out what you want to do next so that you're better able to apply what you learn there. Save your money and choose your school carefully, making sure there will be plenty of people there who will really challenge you. And once you're on campus, find mentors and build important relationships that will help you in the future."

Maggie
From Swing Dancer to Nutritionist

As a child, twenty-eight-year-old Maggie loved dancing. She mastered ballet, jazz, and tap, and as a freshman at the University of

California at Berkeley, she learned Lindy hop, or swing dancing. "I started dancing professionally by my second year of college," she says. "I was traveling around the country and the world to teach and perform Lindy hop, and when I had a death in my family early in my career, dancing offered a wonderful distraction. This was a period in my life in which I lived entirely in the moment. Maybe it was delayed maturation, but I was completely immersed in my dance world and couldn't see farther than that. I progressed faster and faster, and before I knew it, I was paying my rent with my dancing paychecks."

While in the San Francisco area, Maggie kept her skills sharp by dancing socially every night of the week and attending jazz, tap, and hip-hop classes. She gained attention by winning local, regional, national, and international competitions, which in turn drew offers to teach workshops, perform in shows, and judge competitions. As Maggie's profile expanded, she was tapped to coordinate national dance events and found that she had to be skilled politically as well as athletically. "I achieved a certain level of celebrity, and suddenly my words and actions were being repeated through gossip and benign industry discussion," she relates. "As an authority figure, I was held up to different standards, and I had to learn to be cordial with strangers who wanted to talk about dance or to dance with me. It was a lot of responsibility for a young adult, and I didn't always handle it well."

Maggie gradually tired of a dance community that didn't offer her the intellectual stimulation she craved, and her boyfriend at the time encouraged her to aspire to greater things. After considering a variety of options and marrying her source of inspiration, Maggie decided to pursue her interest in nutrition and human behavior. She began a graduate program in nutrition at Columbia University's Teachers College, in New York City. "Having no background in science, I had to take a lot of undergraduate Chem 101–type classes along with my graduate courses in learning theories and social health policy and the like," Maggie explains.

Maggie's biggest challenge was finding common ground with her younger classmates. "I was thriving through intellectual discourse with my graduate peers at Columbia, but meanwhile I was stuck in courses with undergrads who were still drifting or just trying to get by. It was frustrating," she admits. She was intimidated academically as well. "I knew that I didn't have a knack for science, and because of this mind-set, I made a concentrated effort to work really hard and it wasn't as difficult as I thought it would be. When you understand how to think critically and make connections, science is really just a lot of memorization. I'd challenge any scientist to analyze a poem. I think it would be much harder to go from science to humanities than the other way around."

Along with her master's degree, Maggie also completed a professional degree and became a registered dietician. She began working in community health settings, including the United Way of New York City and the Columbia University Head Start program. In the former position, Maggie was a member of the advisory committee responsible for reviewing grant applications for the Eat Well, Play Hard program, and she collaborated with nutrition community members from organizations including the New York State Department of Health. In the latter, she reviewed medical charts, identified nutritional risk factors, and made dietary recommendations for children ages 0–5. She also created a lesson plan for parents to increase toddler fruit and vegetable intake.

Currently a nutrition specialist with Pollock Communications (www.pollock-pr.com), Maggie spends the bulk of her days putting together educational materials for a variety of audiences. "Sometimes I'm writing press releases about key findings from a new research study; other times I'm doing booklets or brochures for patients and health care practitioners," she says. "I spend my mornings scanning *The New York Times* and Google Alerts for news relevant to my food and nutrition clients, which is especially fun on Science Tuesdays and Dining Out Wednesdays."

Maggie thanks her parents for supporting a culture of lifelong learning: "They believed in me and let me make my own choices about academic activities and hobbies." She suggests that prospective students be realistic about why they want to be in school. "Some people go back because they think it's prestigious to have another degree, or they want to delay being a part of real life for a while.

But not all jobs lend themselves to further education, so interview people at different stages of the career you're choosing—including people who went back to school and people who didn't—to see what will work best for you."

And once you've taken the plunge, don't isolate yourself. "Spend the time that isn't specifically used for coursework getting involved at school and working on extra research projects," says Maggie. "Often, simply showing up at events in your academic and professional community will be helpful to your career transition."

Jon
From Ribs Maker to Commodities Trader to Psychology Professor

Jon was always a free spirit. After graduating from high school, he entered the University of Colorado, only to drop out a short while later. He partied, skied, and worked odd jobs. And then, reality called. Jon was out of money, so he moved to Chicago to work for his father, who owned a wholesale meat and poultry company. "The company was founded by my grandfather, and we were known for our St. Louis–style spareribs," says Jon. "I was poised to take over eventually, so I learned the business from the ground up. I handled sales and restaurant purchases and even drove the delivery truck."

In his twenties, though, Jon wasn't the most motivated or responsible employee in the world. "My own father fired me," he admits sheepishly. "Not knowing what else I could do, I decided to take advantage of the fact that my dad had a seat at the Chicago Board of Trade and Mercantile Exchange." Jon entered the whirlwind life of a commodities trader, spending his mornings on the floor speculating on futures prices. "You can make or lose a fortune in an instant," he says. "It was extremely stressful and full of temptations."

Meanwhile, in Jon's absence, his father's ribs company flourished. His partner's son joined the business, and they were bought out—very lucratively—by ConAgra, a global food manufacturer. Jon found himself addicted to nicotine and disenchanted with the world. He didn't know what he wanted to do careerwise, but it continually nagged at him that he didn't have a college degree. "I was in the midst of a full-blown existential crisis, and missed the sense of accomplishment associated with learning," he says. "So I picked myself up and relocated to Minnesota, where I enrolled as a psychology major at the University of Minnesota."

Why the psychology major? "As someone who couldn't control the impulse to smoke, I was intrigued by how the mind works. I wanted to understand my addiction on an intellectual level," he says. On campus, Jon got involved with a laboratory that was conducting smoking research, and was soon getting all A's. "I found that I loved posing questions and then systematically seeking answers to them."

Having returned to college after several years in the workforce, Jon was older than most of his classmates. "This worried me at first, but I gradually began to make friends who were younger, which kept me feeling younger," he says. The years accelerated, and as graduation approached, Jon decided to pursue a Ph.D. at the University of Pittsburgh.

Shortly after arriving in Pennsylvania, Jon married his girlfriend, Rena, and the two prepared for the birth of their first child. It was then that Jon found that he had no choice but to finally quit smoking. "It made me feel terrible to see this overflowing ashtray sitting next to my very pregnant wife," he relates. "And plus, my academic adviser said that in order to be taken seriously as a smoking researcher I would have to give it up." He never picked up a cigarette again.

Jon was in his element in graduate school. "For the first time in my life, I had this sense of self-efficacy, like I was really good at what I was doing. I was able to juggle dozens of things at once without stopping for breath." He began work on his dissertation on the effects of smoking on emotion, and Rena—who worked part-time as a research assistant—was soon pregnant with their second daughter. His parents helped the young family financially until Jon received his degree and entered the job market for a faculty position in clinical psychology.

After a stint at the University of Florida, Jon became tenured at the University of Illinois at Chicago. Today, he is a full professor and co-director of clinical training. "I have my own lab focused on addiction research, and I teach graduate students on methods for clinical intervention and advise them on their careers. I really enjoy the writing aspect of my job, spending a lot of time putting together grants and scientific papers." Jon's crowning achievement is a review of the literature on how smoking affects stress, recently published in the prestigious journal *Psychological Bulletin*.

Clinical psychology is widely known as one of the most competitive academic fields to break into, and Jon was able to do it by taking an honest look at himself and persevering even when he felt insecure. "I made a conscious decision not to live according to the rules of others, and this was at times painful. There were definitely days that I felt like an impostor and was certain I'd never make it in the field," he says.

If you're thinking of going back to school, Jon recommends you view the process as a journey. "It will open up so many paths, but you have to be patient and put in the time." And in academic life, both pre- and post-Ph.D., you must have the self-discipline to be your own boss and set your own hours. "An academic career affords a degree of freedom that you can't experience in a traditional forty-hour-a-week job," Jon says. "No one is watching you, and you're given just enough rope to hang yourself if you're not careful. I've seen people do it, and it's not pretty."

One thing's for sure: You'll only make it if something inside you yearns for that extra body of knowledge that an advanced degree brings. "No one goes into clinical psychology to get rich," says Jon. "You have to love it. And I do."

Robin
From Sewage Plant Worker to Information Technology Administrator

Robin grew up in Detroit, a manufacturing town. In and out of college, she took local jobs in various manufacturing plants. "I made brakes and plastic wrapping before getting a good job—one that pays well and includes vacation and medical benefits—at the city of Detroit's wastewater treatment plant," she says. "I worked in various positions there at the oxygen plant and at the vacuum presses, cleaning the water tanks and hauling waste to landfills."

The work was a horrible experience for Robin, both mentally and physically. "I spent much of my time holding my breath to keep from swallowing the stench of raw sewage. The work was physically demanding and I tore cartilage in my knees, pulled muscles in my back, and pinched a nerve in my neck." Robin knew she didn't belong there, and questioned why she was working a menial job instead of building a career. Robin often shared her desire to do something more with her life, and one day her partner called her bluff. "She signed me up for an interview with a local organization called Focus: HOPE [FH]. FH had been created as a nonprofit after the 1967 Detroit riots to provide services to the community. By the time I applied, it had grown into a leading program for machinist training that included an opportunity to gain a bachelor's degree of science in engineering."

Robin's interview went well, and when the recruiter called the next day and asked if she would consider a brand-new information technology (IT) program, she was elated. "I was much more interested in learning computers than die-cast machines, so I said yes. I left the sewage plant and never looked back." Her first course in basic computer skills lasted thirty days, and she went on to Computer Learning Center, an accelerated vocational school. "I spent the next seven months learning computer network engineering, and got my first full-time job right after graduation working for Hospice of Michigan as a network technician." Handling end-user support, PC builds, and server administration, Robin was a long way from the plant.

In less than a year, Robin was offered a position as a network administrator for a construction company, but her appetite to increase her skill set was voracious. She enrolled in the Cisco Network Academy program and got her Cisco Certified Network Associate certification. Robin now had certifications in networking technologies such as MCSE, CCNA, A+, CAN, and Network +, but she found herself shut out of desirable opportunities because she still hadn't obtained a bachelor's degree. Robin was on a roll, so, while working full-time, she began a bachelor's of science program in information technology at Capella, an accredited university geared to adult learners. Pretty soon, she was earning a 4.0 GPA and had snagged a lucrative scholarship.

Although Robin had achieved what many thought was an enviable situation, the life as an IT administrator had its hardships. "Endless days of demands and dissatisfaction always outweighed any praise," she says. "People tend to concentrate on the negative and take the positive for granted, and high stress and late nights were a common occurrence." As an African American woman, she also struggled constantly with gender and race discrimination. "Information technology is a white, male-dominated industry. It is filled with men and boys whose egos are the size of basketballs and have the social skills of gnats. I am often challenged on my way of resolving an issue when my male counterparts are not, and it's difficult to be heard without shouting."

Nevertheless, Robin has continued to look for ways to grow. Through a 24/7 connection with other "geeks," she stays abreast of rapidly changing technologies. She has acquired a working knowledge of good documentation and preventive maintenance, and has mastered the art of teamwork and leadership. "I've realized that there is no secret to success. The answers are usually right there in front of you if you're just willing to listen," she says.

Robin now lives in New Hampshire and works as a technical support engineer for IBM's Rational ClearCase software product. She has found that she really enjoys helping people, so the regular customer contact is exciting. "The product is very complex and it takes a year to generally understand how it works and then several more years to be proficient in supporting or using it," says Robin. "Though I will be leaving IBM shortly to move closer to my family, it has provided a great technical learning experience. I was able to build stronger problem analysis skills that I can use in other areas of my life."

To other career changers who are considering returning to school, Robin says: "Going to school is more difficult than working because each week brings a new set of assignment challenges. It's not for the faint of heart." She believes that you must be both driven and focused to make a major change. "Perseverance is key.

The thought of quitting often entered my mind but I didn't let it get too comfortable there. There were always more reasons to quit than to finish—I'm tired, it's hard, I don't have time for friends—but I just wouldn't do it no matter what obstacle I faced."

Gregg
From Submarine Commander to IT Executive to Judge Advocate General

Gregg always knew he wanted to go to college, but money was a factor from the beginning. He began his university career at the University of Michigan in the highly regarded Reserve Officers' Training Corps (ROTC) program, but that scholarship couldn't support him. He briefly joined the navy in order to earn more money for school, and then resumed his education at Eastern Michigan University, where he graduated with a major in computer science and a minor in mathematics.

Still with the ROTC program, Gregg began training as a submarine nuclear engineer, taking courses in subjects such as thermodynamics and particle physics and designing nuclear prototypes. "It was grueling," he remembers. "There was one six-month period where I worked a hundred hours a week." Gregg considered becoming a pilot, but that path seemed static. He looked forward to the constant change and excitement of life aboard a sub, and felt that he could use his education to eventually work for the Nuclear Regulatory Commission or one of several nuclear advocacy groups.

After his submarine training was complete, Gregg's first position was as a chemical and radiological assistant. Assigned to be on board the sub for three years, he was handed a leadership role immediately. "In that job, I learned the difference between a manager and a leader. Managers get things done, while leaders teach others to get things done," Gregg says. "A sub is a high-stress work environment. You spend more time with your colleagues than you do with your family, and you can't get away when things get difficult. At the same time, if you have the social skills to make it, your colleagues eventually become like brothers."

Although the twenty-something Gregg did well on his first tour, he hungered for a greater challenge. He decided to leverage his background in energy and computer science and apply for a position with NASA. "After all, space shuttles are not that different from subs," he muses. Gregg made it to the final round of consideration, but failed the hearing test that was part of the physical exam. He was devastated. "Careerwise, it was a very tough time, but in my personal life, I'd just met my wife and she was an incredible source of support."

Soured by his experience with NASA, Gregg left the navy and took a series of private-sector information technology (IT) jobs while his wife, Mary, was attending nursing school. When she graduated, the couple moved to San Diego, and she was soon pregnant with their first child, Anna. An experienced IT manager by this point, Gregg began working for CSC, an IT contractor that provides services to the Space and Naval Warfare Systems Command (SPAWAR). After launching the Help Desk for the Navy's Internet, Gregg was offered a high-level position as deputy director. "I realized I was going down a certain road, and when I pictured what my life as an IT executive would be like in twenty, thirty years, I wasn't sure I liked what I saw," Gregg admits. "I wanted to do something that would fulfill me and satisfy my intellectual curiosity. I kept up on current events and loved to talk about politics. Back on the sub, one of my dearest friends called my constant stream of factoids 'news McNuggets.' He said that I was the person who knew something about everything."

Gregg had been intrigued by the law from a young age, but it was an interest he'd always kept filed away. "When I told my wife I wanted to go to law school, she thought I'd lost my mind. I had to admit to her that I didn't have a plan, and that I just wanted to keep learning." Gregg moved the family to Chicago, where he enrolled at the Chicago-Kent College of Law. "I told myself I just needed to bear down for a few years, but it was very hard. I went from a good salary to no salary, and had taken on tons of debt in the midst of having one child to support and another on the way," he says. "I commuted four hours a day to school, and, as a thirty-something, often felt out of place among the younger students. But the experience was valuable, because I learned that I could make any situation work. My maturity from having been out in the world balanced out the fact that I wasn't as energetic as the kids in my classes."

As law school drew to a close, Gregg prepared to take a job at a large Chicago firm. But the events of September 11, 2001, convinced him otherwise. He lost a friend who was working at the Pentagon that day, and he realized that he missed the camaraderie of the Navy. Gregg applied for a position as a judge advocate general (JAG), a process that involved passing the bar, completing an orientation, and taking several weeks of Navy-related courses such as military criminal law, government contract law, and international relations. As one of the fifty JAGs accepted that year, Gregg filled a role as a staff judge advocate and legal adviser to Sub Squad 15, stationed at the naval base in Guam. Is Gregg's job like the television show *JAG*? Sort of. "My job includes working with public affairs to put out a news release on hosting a foreign sub, telling departments how to spend money, managing ethical issues like the proper use of government vehicles, and advising the navy on orders violations and cases of dereliction of duty," he tells us. There's never a dull moment because, as Gregg says, the military is held to a higher standard than the civilian world and therefore has a spotlight on its actions. "It's not unusual for me to get a call at three A.M. because so-and-so is in jail."

Although Gregg occasionally misses the formal school environment, he finds that he's still always learning. He's currently volunteering as a special assistant United States attorney—prosecuting cases such as drunken driving, in federal court. He also hopes to seek a specialty in environmental law. To those who are pushed toward career change by a desire to know more about the world, Gregg says to beware of stagnation. "Don't worry about how old you are, and ask the right questions of the right people," he advises. "I'm just a common guy who didn't take no for an answer and figured out the right thing to do. You can, too."

☞ **Self-Reflection: Is Learning Your Motivation?**
• Were you more than a little sad when your schooling came to an end?

- Do you find yourself watching History and Discovery channel shows purely because you're interested in the subject matter?
- Do you actually read the salesy emails sent to you by traditional or online schools?
- Have you often felt mentally understimulated, as if you aren't making good use of your intellectual capabilities, in your current job?
- Have you taken advantage of several professional development opportunities offered by your employer?
- Do you enjoy perusing the industry literature that gets passed around the office?
- Are you jealous of your friends who have made the decision to obtain a degree?
- Has your family threatened to take matters into their own hands and sign you up for a degree program?
- Is it easy for you to envision taking classes by day and studying by night?
- Do you have confidence in your desire and ability to pursue a career in which it will be necessary for you to return to school?

👍 If you answered "Yes" to two or more of these questions, you may be headed back to school sooner than you think. Before you start those applications, though, arm yourself with the information in the next section.

☞ Putting the Change to Work

Assess your situation: You may have heard the term *professional student,* and people who enjoy school often pursue additional education without a clear goal in mind. However, if you're planning to use your desire to learn as a jumping-off point to a new career, you should first perform a cost/benefit analysis to determine how a degree program will help you break in. Check out the Bureau of Labor Statistics' *Occupational Outlook Handbook* to see what education is needed for your chosen path, and then map out a plan for how you'll use the training and degree to facilitate it. When you return to school after a few years in the workforce, it might not be as easy as it was when you were eighteen, for now you might be balancing a spouse, children, work, community responsibilities, or even the care of elderly parents or grandparents. You should determine, up front, if it's realistic to fit school into your life at this time.

Seek the support of your family: According to Al Siebert and Mary Karr in their book *The Adult Student's Guide to Survival and Success,* you should talk honestly with your family about your prospective role as a student. Explain why going to school is important to you, ask about their concerns, and listen with understanding. You should be very specific about the type of support you will require. For example, will you need to move back in with your parents for a brief time in order to save money? If you're married, will you need undisturbed time to study or help with household chores? When your loved ones are helpful and go out of their way to assist you in your educational goals, show them thanks and appreciation.

Select schools and/or programs: Depending on your anticipated career trajectory, different educational options may be open to you, including:

- *Associate's degree:* known as the entry-level of college education; earned in a two-year program emphasizing general studies.
- *Bachelor of arts (B.A.):* earned in a four-year program emphasizing humanities and arts courses.
- *Bachelor of science (B.S.):* earned in a four-year program emphasizing science and mathematics courses.
- *Master's degree (M.A. or M.S.):* earned after the B.A. or B.S.; involves writing a thesis at the conclusion of approximately two years of coursework in a particular discipline.
- *Doctorate of philosophy (Ph.D.) or education (Ed.D.):* usually earned after the master's degree with a number of years of advanced, graduate-level seminar work and a doctoral thesis based on original research.
- *Juris doctor (J.D.):* earned after the completion of a three-year law school program.
- *Doctor of medicine (M.D.):* earned after the completion of a four-year medical school program and typically followed by a period of clinical training in the form of an internship and/or residency.

As a result of your research, you may learn that returning to school for a formal degree is unnecessary. Instead, you might consider short-term training workshops in your new field, a certificate or vocational program offered through a local community college or university extension program, or a retraining program through a career center or outplacement service that focuses on the acquisition of a specific group of skills. If becoming a full-time student isn't conducive to your lifestyle, many educational institutions accommodate part-time schedules in which classes are held in the evenings and on the weekends. The only drawback is that it will usually take you twice the amount of time to finish the program.

Once you've decided on the type of program, scour the Internet and reference books for the schools that offer what you need and make a list of your top choices. Every institution on your short list should be accredited, which means that it has been independently evaluated and has met standards of quality set by the U.S. Department of Education and the Council for Higher Education Accreditation. Long-term, formal degree programs should be vetted by interviews with current faculty members or students before you apply. What should you ask in these conversations? MsMoney .com provides these sample questions for those considering business school:

- What are the backgrounds/qualifications of the faculty?
- What is the student-to-faculty ratio? How accessible are faculty members?
- What percentage of applicants is accepted? What is their background?
- What is a standard course load? How long do students typically take to graduate?
- What is the condition of the physical facilities (classrooms, libraries, etc.)?
- Is the curriculum targeted at a particular industry or purpose (high tech, entrepreneurship, manufacturing, etc.), and, if so, does the academic emphasis fit your interests?

- What job placement resources are available? Which companies recruit on campus?
- What percentage of students is placed in jobs?

Consider distance learning: The Distance Education and Training Council, via Back to College (www.back2college.com), claims that four million students are currently taking college courses through distance education. Distance learning, which involves coursework outside the traditional classroom environment, can be very convenient for those who are balancing work and family responsibilities. Through public and private universities, as well as institutions such as the University of Phoenix (www.phoenix.edu), Capella (www.capella.edu), and DeVry (www.devry.edu), which specialize in distance education, you can use the variety of multimedia tools available via the Internet to simulate in-person lectures and tests. The advantages of distance degrees include their relatively lower cost and the fact that you can usually complete assignments on your own schedule. The downside is that you must be completely self-motivated to make distance learning work, and you'll likely miss the camaraderie of being surrounded by fellow students. As with traditional degree programs, you can identify distance learning options by searching online—just make sure the institution is accredited.

Plan for the costs: Higher education is indeed expensive, but the situation is not as bad as you might think. Back to College and the College Board recently reported that 65 percent of students at four-year schools pay tuition of under $9K a year, and 56 percent pay between $3K and $6K. Additionally, 62 percent of full-time students receive grants. Aid in the form of grants and tax benefits averaged about $2.2K per student at two-year public schools, more than $3.1K at public four-year schools, and $9K at private four-year schools.

You can calculate the approximate costs for obtaining an additional degree by inputting the schools you're interested in and the number of years you'll be attending on the Princeton Review (www.princetonreview.com), CNN Money (money.cnn.com), and Yahoo! Finance (finance.yahoo.com) websites. Scared by the number? If you plan to keep working while you're in school, your company may have a tuition assistance program of which you can take advantage. You can also use online scholarship search services such as www.finaid.org and www.scholarships.com, visit your bank of choice to learn about low-interest loans, and work with your accountant to leverage education tax credits such as the Lifetime Learning Credit. Don't assume that you won't qualify for financial aid, since many sources are offered regardless of financial need or credit history. Most federal and state aid programs don't have age limits, and if you're a single parent you may be automatically eligible. As soon as you make the decision to return to school, submit the Free Application for Federal Student Aid (FAFSA) to see what assistance Uncle Sam can provide!

Take standardized tests: If a bachelor's of arts or science is what you're after, Back to College tells us that many institutions grant credit through standardized exams such as the College Level Examination Program (CLEP) and Defense Activity for Non-Traditional Education Support (DANTES), which may be taken in several subject areas. Graduate level education normally requires that you take one of four major admissions tests:

- *Graduate Record Examination (GRE):* Given in seven parts, this test scores verbal, quantitative, and analytical abilities.
- *Graduate Management Admission Test (GMAT):* This test has nine sections that score verbal, mathematical, and analytical writing skills.
- *Medical College Admission Test (MCAT):* This nine-hour test assesses problem solving and critical thinking skills, as well as knowledge of scientific concepts.
- *Law School Admission Test (LSAT):* This competitive, five-part test lasts half a day and measures acquired reading and verbal reasoning skills.

Strong scores on these tests will be critical for gaining admission to your school of choice, and also tend to be helpful for financial aid purposes. Be sure to leave plenty of preparation time before test day, calling on resources such as www.testpreview.com, www.mba.com, and www.kaplan.com to learn what to expect, access study tools, and take practice exams.

Prepare your applications: Many applications can be completed online, but, depending on the program, you may need to call schools you've attended to obtain copies of your official transcripts. Letters of recommendation are also a common requirement. As an adult returning to school, letters from current or former employers are best. Do not use friends or family members, and make sure you give prospective references an adequate amount of direction and notice. Most degree programs in higher education ask that you write an essay, or personal statement, as part of the application process. Essays should be tailored to each program, and according to Tara Kuther, the graduate school guide for About.com, they often ask you to address areas such as:

- *Career plans:* What are your long-term career goals? Where do you see yourself ten years from now?
- *Academic interests:* What would you like to study? Which professors in the department would you like to work with?
- *Personal experience:* Is there anything in your background that you think is relevant to your application?

Your personal essay is a story that tells the admissions committee who you are and what you can offer. While the questions posed will differ by program, the general challenge is to introduce yourself and describe your potential as a successful candidate. Kuther suggests preparing for your essay before you start writing, and taking the time to think about the central theme asked and how it corresponds to your personal qualities and experiences. Emphasize your accomplishments, showcase your motivation, and don't be redundant.

Decide on your course load: It's a smart idea to map out, in advance, what classes you're going to take and when. The following are general guidelines for the length of time it takes to complete various degrees:

- *Certificate program* (culinary arts, computer technology, childhood education, real estate, travel, etc.): one year
- *Associate's degree:* two years for full-time students
- *Bachelor's degree:* four years for full-time students

- *Master's degree:* two-plus years for full-time students
- *Doctoral degree:* four-plus years for full-time students
- *Law degree:* three years for full-time students
- *Medical degree:* five years for full-time students

The experts at Back to College advise that a full-time college course load is around twelve hours a week, although some students take up to eighteen credit hours. Part-time study is generally one to eleven credit hours a week. Independent study encompasses three hours a week for each credit hour. For your first semester back, consider attending part-time and registering for just one or two courses, especially if you plan to keep working. Much as you might be invigorated by learning, your enthusiasm will quickly flag if you take on too much.

Assuage age concerns: Back to College and the Association of Nontraditional Students in Higher Education report that students who are over twenty-five make up 47 percent of the new and returning student population on many of today's college campuses, and recent statistics from Back to College and the U.S. Department of Education indicate that adult students are the fastest-growing educational demographic. Nevertheless, unless they're in graduate programs that encourage a few years in the workforce first, many older students feel insecure about taking classes alongside people who are five or ten years younger. They worry about fitting in and finding study partners to whom they can relate. You should know, though, that instructors view older students as some of the most gifted and motivated in their classrooms. They, as well as younger classmates, will look to you to provide the wisdom of experience, and real-world applications for what is being taught. So share freely and proudly!

Practice good learning habits: According to Siebert and Karr in their book *The Adult Student's Guide to Survival and Success,* research into student success shows that students who consistently do well in their courses:

- Find out at the first class when all tests will be held and when papers or projects are due
- Attend all classes and prepare for them in advance

- Ask good questions of the instructor
- Take good lecture notes
- Study regularly and set specific study goals each time
- Mix study subjects and motivate themselves by interspersing rewards
- Hand in coursework on time
- Prepare for tests by writing practice tests and examining examples of old tests
- Work well with other students on group projects
- Use up-to-date sources for papers and solicit feedback from the instructor on drafts
- Organize their time well via to-do lists and calendars

Fortunately, the Web has made efficient studying easier than ever. Tools you might want to check out if you're going back to school include:

- Easy Notes (www.rawos.com): Manages your class notes in electronic form, integrating sticky notes as well as calendar references. Each note supports rich-text formatting that is recognized by nearly all text editors. You can import and export files, or "pin" your notes on your desktop.
- MindManager (www.mindjet.com): Provides a dynamic online environment to brainstorm project and paper ideas, generate and visually capture coherent thoughts, and collaborate with groups.
- QuickMath (www.quickmath.com): Offers a free online calculator that solves equations and completes algebra and calculus problems. When you submit a question to QuickMath, the answer is displayed on your browser within seconds.
- ScholarSuite (www.meteortech.com): Creates quick outlines for your papers, automatically writes bibliographies in the MLA and APA formats, and keeps all of your reference information organized electronically.
- Web Reading Made Easy (www.xemantex.com): Allows you to obtain dictionary meanings for words and comprehend the

gist of online content without referring to Web or hardcover dictionaries.

Form a support group: Returning to school after years in the workforce is a challenging transition even if you're sure you're doing the right thing. You can bond with other students who understand what you're going through by forming a support group of five to eight people. Plan regular meetings at a place where you can talk comfortably with one another about what brought you to the decision to continue your education. Conduct the sessions so that each person feels heard, and if some of you are interested in collaborating academically, form offshoot study groups as well. Leverage online technology and/or social networking to keep in touch on an everyday basis.

Be visible: Most of the folks I spoke to who received additional education as adult students told me that the network they built as a result was the single most important benefit of returning to school. So even though you'll be quite busy with your coursework, you should make an effort to get to know your fellow students, professors, and other faculty, for these are the people who may provide valuable employment and collaboration opportunities in your future career as well as advice and friendship while you're still in school. Make a list of everyone in your department and try to establish a personal connection with each individual. In particular, your academic adviser is someone with whom you should develop a strong mentor/mentee relationship. The experience he's gained from years in the field and connections he has forged will prove helpful to you in the long term.

You should also join clubs and third-party organizations on campus that are related to your area of study, and participate in their committees and events. Attend conferences and volunteer to help people you've met with special projects or research endeavors. When attending an industry event, dress professionally even if you're a full-time student who normally wears jeans and sneakers. Exchange business cards and e-contact information with everyone you meet, and be sure to follow up with an invitation for lunch or coffee. A second meeting will ensure they don't forget who you are!

☞ Exercise: Planning for Your Education

- Write down the major reason you're considering going back to school. Will more formal education help you realize your personal learning and/or career goals? If not, what other avenues might you pursue to achieve them?

- Take stock of your education so far. What degrees, or how many college credits do you have, and do you have any work experience that might count toward a degree?

- Research and draft a paragraph summary of the typical academic plan for someone who wants to transition into your career of choice.

- Write down the first three steps you will need to take to put your plan in motion (determine appropriate institutions, take preliminary coursework, procure financial aid, etc.) and talk them over with your family.

- Evaluate the impact that returning to school will have on your financial situation and sketch a budget that takes into account school costs and reduced income.

- Devise a theoretical weekday schedule that would combine work, school, and family responsibilities.

☞ **Resource Toolkit**

Websites

Back to College: www.back2college.com
College Board: www.collegeboard.com
Education Index: www.educationindex.com
FinAid: www.finaid.org
GradSchools.com: www.gradschools.com
Internet Public Library: www.ipl.org
Test Prep Review: www.testprepreview.com
U.S. Department of Education: www.ed.gov

Books

Bear's Guide to Earning Degrees by Distance Learning (Mariah Bear and Thomas Nixon)
Your MBA Game Plan: Proven Strategies for Getting into the Top Business Schools (Omari Bouknight and Scott Shrum)
College Board Guide to Getting Financial Aid (College Board)
Get into Graduate School: A Strategic Approach for Master's and Doctoral Candidates (Kaplan)
Law School Confidential: A Complete Guide to the Law School Experience (Robert Miller)
The Adult Student's Guide to Survival and Success (Al Siebert and Mary Karr)
Adult Students: An Insider's Guide to Getting into College (Gen and Kelly Tanabe)
U.S. News Ultimate College Guide (*U.S. News & World Report*)

Money

> When I was young, I used to think that money was the most
> important thing in life. Now that I'm old, I know it is.
> —Oscar Wilde, playwright

The pursuit of money is the rationale for a lot of things we do in life,
including changing our careers. This is apparently with good reason. In a 2008 study, University of Pennsylvania researchers Betsey
Stevenson and Justin Wolfers found that money indeed tends to
bring happiness. The study was based on Gallup polls done around
the world and clearly showed that life satisfaction is highest in the
richest countries.

If you're reading this book, you probably have enough money to
support your basic needs, and hopefully a little extra to occasionally
indulge in the fun things in life—like eating out at a five-star restaurant or flying down to Costa Rica to go zip-lining. It may be the case,
though, that your current job doesn't provide you with the income
you require. The economy has hit more than a few rough patches
recently, and in many cities, costs are increasing astronomically.
Maybe you need more money so that you can support a certain lifestyle or better provide for your family, maybe you want to increase
your status among your peer group, maybe you want a means to
give back to society and donate to philanthropic causes you care
about, or maybe you simply want your income to reflect the daily
effort you put into your work. A bigger paycheck won't solve all your
problems—or the world's—but it can certainly make things a lot
easier.

I've sometimes said that I haven't based my career decisions on
money, and it's true that I did voluntarily step away from a six-figure

salary as a marketing communications vice president to pursue my career as an author. However, I also made a conscious decision to write a certain type of book based on the income I could derive from it, and that's why my niche is now business instead of fiction. Writing career advice books also facilitates alternative revenue streams for me, such as corporate and conference speaking engagements. Since I'm not independently wealthy and my husband makes a modest salary as a professor of psychology, money will simply always be a factor when I decide how to steer my career.

Despite the popularity of instant-millionaire game shows and get-rich-quick schemes that blanket the Internet, most people are willing to work hard to make more money, and changing careers strategically is often a good way to ensure that your endeavors are funneled in a productive direction. And by the way, it's a myth that you have to start your own business to earn a comfortable living. This is an approach that works well for some, but plenty of folks do just fine working in salaried positions in large organizations.

This chapter will introduce several individuals who customized careers that allowed them to achieve their financial aspirations and will close with some important advice and considerations when money *is* an object, including how to get out of debt, how to select a profitable field, and how to hire a financial adviser who will make your money work for you.

Randy
From Writer to Tennis Promoter to Sponsorship Salesperson

At the University of Georgia, Randy was the greatest tennis player never to win a match. "If Georgia was the Notre Dame of tennis, then I was Rudy," he says. "I'd been playing since age five, but I wasn't good enough to be on that team. My sophomore year, though, I convinced them to let me play anyway. I was 0 and 7."

Randy thought he might become a sports journalist when he graduated from college, so he decided to use his tennis connections to get some writing experience. He covered the tennis team for one of the school's newspapers and helped out in the team's pressroom.

He even managed to score some clips reporting college tennis for large media outlets such as the *Chicago Sun-Times*. "I was the big dog on campus, and everyone knew who I was," he says.

Randy's impressive résumé led him to become one of the only journalism majors to get a job right out of school. He was hired as the sports editor for the stats page at Georgia's *Daily News*. "The paper was owned by *The New York Times*, and at the time was trying to compete with *The Atlanta Journal-Constitution*," Randy explains. "I had outscooped my rival a lot while I was in college, and they liked that." Unfortunately, the job paid just twelve thousand dollars a year, not enough money for Randy to live on. Randy saw more senior reporters and editors toiling endless hours for no money, and he didn't want to be in their shoes. "I knew that it would take a long time to be covering the Super Bowl, and in the meantime, journalism was simply not going to pay for the lifestyle that I wanted."

At the age of twenty-three, Randy quit his job without another in hand, and moved back home to New Canaan, Connecticut. His lack of planning incurred the ire of his father, and the two argued frequently. "I made a little money freelancing, but I needed a career, so I took an inventory of my skills," Randy says. "Being a journalism major and then a reporter and editor, I knew how to write well. I could still hear my professors chiding me to spell this word correctly, or put that punctuation mark in the right place. I had also developed good news instincts. I knew how to find the drama and the human interest in a story, and could give it to journalists in the right format."

As a result of his exploration, Randy thought that public relations would be an ideal fit and decided to use his tennis knowledge to break into the field. He volunteered at the Volvo International Tennis Tournament in New Haven, and through his contacts there was offered a paid gig as a media assistant for the U.S. Open. During this time, Randy heard that the U.S. Tennis Association was consolidating their offices in nearby White Plains, New York. Randy called the organization repeatedly and spent many a night biting his nails and waiting to hear back. He eventually landed a PR manager position, which proved to be windfall. "To say there were tremendous perks would be an understatement," says Randy. "I orchestrated events and interviews with all the tennis greats, including a young Lindsay Davenport. I was the press officer for three Olympic Games and traveled with the U.S. Davis Cup team all around the world."

Randy had as good a PR job as he could get, and he had achieved his financial objectives with a salary that approached six figures. But he felt a little disillusionment nipping at his heels. "In the world of tennis PR, there aren't a lot of options in case you get fired," he explains. "Plus, I lived in Manhattan, and had pretty much reached the income cap for a PR guy. It's the classic case of the billionaire who wants the bigger plane."

Randy wasn't sure what to do, so he saw a career counselor. "Ninety percent of the session was useless, but he did say one important thing that has stayed with me. When you cross a river, you don't just appear on the other side. You look for the rock in the middle that allows you to get across, and a career transition is the same way," he says. Randy determined that his rock was sponsorship sales, something that would leverage his sports experience and also allow him to increase his income. He and a former intern got their start by putting together a PR and sponsorship plan for the National Lacrosse League. "I have to be honest, it wasn't that easy. You face a crazy amount of rejection in sponsorships, and you have to be willing to keep calling back at different times, to stay on top of it." Gradually, Randy expanded his client base and was able to form his own company, Leverage Agency (www.leverageagency .com). The business has done so well that Randy has been able to dabble in publishing, his first title a top-selling biography of Roger Federer.

Randy claims that he made all of this happen through sheer will. "I believe that if you don't get something you want, well, you just didn't want it bad enough," he says. "I've been willing to work for free. I've tried hard to build a brand that people remember. I've read tons of inspirational business books. In order to make money, I've had to take risks. Even if you're afraid, you just have to do it, because even if you fail, it won't be as bad as you think."

Michelle
From Theater Producer to Nonprofit Education Designer
to Media Entrepreneur

In order to pay for her education, Michelle always held extra jobs. Starting in high school, you could find her doing children's birthday parties dressed as a princess, pirate, or Barbie. Michelle developed a love for her performing, and, in her early twenties, earned a bachelor of fine arts in children's theater from DePaul University in Chicago. When she graduated, Michelle took a job producing plays for Call to Action, a nonprofit organization with the goal of reforming the Catholic Church. This was an issue close to her heart, for Michelle was molested by a neighbor and when she confided in the priest at her Catholic school, was simply ordered to say a few Hail Mary prayers and ask for guidance. "Working with Call to Action's Performing Arts Ministry and producing plays about Dorothy Day and St. Augustine's mistress was right up my alley," says Michelle. "We marketed our performances to churches and spiritual communities around the country, which in turn raised money to host us. In providing a traveling troupe that offered inspiration, education, and political change, Call to Action allowed me to do authentic work that had the same influence over communities that theater did back in the Middle Ages."

Michelle loved her job and thought she would thrive in the Chicago theater scene for the rest of her life. But her boyfriend wanted to move to Louisville, Kentucky, and Michelle's enterprising love soon found her a job creating early childhood curricula for the Little People's Workshop. The company provided day-care centers and preschools with developmentally appropriate learning programs that made use of puppets, flannel toys, and daily activity sheets. Michelle won several awards for her work, and one program that she produced with a large team of artists and educators was recognized by *Earlychildhood NEWS*.

Unfortunately, scandal and financial struggles plagued the well-intentioned organization, and it eventually went bankrupt. "Out of the ashes, a new nonprofit formed called RISE [Resources and Instruction for Staff Excellence]," relates Michelle. "I was their first employee and their main project manager, and we launched TV training networks and national programs for the National Head Start Association and the National Association for the Education of Young Children."

Then, one morning, Michelle woke up with an irresistible desire to pursue her education. "I might have been in a position of power at my job, but I was not as respected because of my level of schooling," she says. "In the education world, if you don't have 'letters' after your name, you are viewed differently." Michelle resigned from RISE to pursue a master's degree in human development at Pacific Oaks College in Pasadena, California. She also began a series of personal growth and development programs with global leadership training provider Landmark Education (www.landmarkeducation.com).

Now in her thirties, Michelle learned a great deal about herself as she completed her coursework. She realized that she had chosen a career in education largely due to her father's emphasis on it, and that she was naturally attracted to business ventures that allowed for independent cash flow. "I began to see that money wasn't something evil people pursued," says Michelle. "I'd always been community service–oriented, but now I recognized that securing funds for a business that I controlled would allow me to make a difference in the lives of huge numbers of people." Michelle also discovered a passion for adventure. During time off from RISE, she'd enjoyed a job as a rafting guide. "I learned at Landmark that I thrive on risk of all kinds—business and personal risk as well as hucking myself off class-five white water." Alongside her husband, a fellow extreme athlete, Michelle started to undertake more frequent outdoor journeys. She needed a job that would allow her to try her hand at rivers around the world.

Michelle decided to start her own media business, but she needed success to come quickly. "My six-figure student loan debt lit a fire under my seat and led me to seek a much higher pay bracket," she remembers. True to her risk-taking nature, Michelle moved to the Great Smoky Mountains of North Carolina with her new business partner before her plans were fully fleshed out. She had taken courses with the U.S. Small Business Administration and SCORE during grad school, and now supplemented her income by waiting tables at night.

The businesses that were born out of Michelle's need to make enough money to support her causes and lifestyle were Wasabi Publicity, Inc. (www.wasabipublicity.com) and Blue Kangaroo. Wasabi Publicity represents people who make a difference and Blue Kangaroo is a technology firm. "Although there are pros and cons to virtual businesses, they give me the freedom to work and play intensely," says Michelle. "Also, the setup allowed me to work while caring for my father during the last few months of his life."

Sometimes, Michelle has to explain to her mother why she takes so many risks. "I don't do it to escape life, but rather to prevent life from escaping me," she says. "I've also learned to go with the flow, which is hard for a type-A person to do. But when I intentionally release and stop getting in my own way, I find that the results and the money come rushing in."

As her ventures have grown, Michelle has also mastered skills associated with running lucrative businesses. "In a service business, active listening is much more important than talking, and I have learned to give great phone," Michelle says. "Also, it's my belief that you can't earn a lot of money if you're disorganized, especially with financial documentation. If you have a stack of paper at your home or office, that's money down the drain because it represents action not taken. Clean up that freakin' paper and get moving!"

Michelle's ultimate goal in forming several self-sustaining companies and multiple streams of income is to retire early and "suck the marrow out of life before I die." She and her husband plan to tour South America by motorbike, so lately Michelle can be found tooling around the Blue Ridge Mountains on her dual-sport.

Jonathan
From Insurance Adjuster to Personal Injury Attorney

Growing up with a father who ran several successful businesses, thirty-four-year-old Jonathan never thought he'd work in insurance. But in his last year of college, majoring in economics at California State University, Jonathan was playing indoor soccer when he met a woman who worked at Prudential. "I talked to her about my job search, and she said they were hiring," he remembers. "I submitted my résumé and went on the interview, and next thing I knew, I had the job." At Prudential, Jonathan started as an adjuster trainee and was promoted to adjuster within six months. The job involved doing research to apply the facts of a particular case to the relevant insurance policy and determine how much is paid on a claim. According to Jonathan, doing it well is an art.

Jonathan was married at twenty-three, and it was important to him to begin saving for his future family. However, his salary at Prudential didn't cut it because the company only handled personal insurance. "To make money, I needed to handle commercial claims," he explains. "Commercial adjusters are paid better because there is much more at stake for the company—we're talking millions in payout as opposed to thousands."

Jonathan applied for a job at CIGNA, where he would have the opportunity to handle both personal and commercial claims. While he learned a lot of about different industries working at CIGNA, Jonathan gradually realized that his profession had a cap on how far he could move up. "The trend was to reduce the number of experienced adjusters and replace them with younger employees without college degrees," he says. "They could be paid much less, and new computer programs could help them do the work."

Jonathan also realized he had an inherent interest in law. At CIGNA, he worked closely with attorneys to settle claims for people and organizations that were being sued, and it was his favorite part of the job. He decided to apply to law school at the University of the Pacific in California, but much to his dismay, CIGNA would not pay for it. Jonathan took a job at an international insurance firm that allowed him to work from home and attend school at night.

Jonathan's experience at the new firm further cemented his desire to leave the insurance world. "I had to spend six weeks in Houston handling a claim for a client," he relates. "I was away from my family and friends, and it was a terrible ordeal. The summer was hot, the city smelled bad, the people I worked with were unfriendly, and I even got a gun pulled on me once." Jonathan also noticed a philosophical change in the way insurance companies conducted business. "All of a sudden, the goal was not to pay a fair and reasonable amount, but to pay as little as you could get away with and delay as long as possible, hoping that people would just give up."

After receiving his law degree, Jonathan took a job at a firm that represented insurance companies. "The transition was relatively easy, because I could bring in clients I knew from when I was working in insurance," he says. But even though he was making more money now, Jonathan saw that it wasn't enough. He and his wife had adopted three boys from New York, and they found the costs astronomical. When the oldest was diagnosed with autism and Jonathan wanted to provide him with the best treatment available, he knew he had to take control of his financial future. He resigned from the law firm on a Friday and opened his own personal injury practice on the following Monday.

As he undertook the process of launching his own legal operation, which included getting a physical address, ordering supplies, applying for malpractice insurance, paying dues to the state bar association, and generating buzz and referrals, Jonathan found that his childhood experiences helping out his father's businesses came in handy. "For example, I learned about parting ways with people when I was sixteen and my dad's top sales manager quit. Watching my dad chat with his factory workers and dine with clients, I also observed how to treat people at all levels respectfully," says Jonathan. "By the time I was in high school, I had a solid understanding of things like budgeting and managing expenses. I basically had a B.A. in running a business."

Jonathan's firm, the Law Offices of Jonathan G. Stein (www .jonathangstein.com), is thriving. "My wife says I have 'damsel-in-distress syndrome,' and it's true that I love my job because I get to help people. I spend my days talking to clients and adverse parties like debt collectors, mortgage companies, and other attorneys. Occasionally, we'll go to court. One of my current clients, for instance, has a son who was hit by a drunk driver, and I'm dealing with both the automobile accident aspect as well as the criminal prosecution aspect."

Now that Jonathan is on his own, he's much more hands-on, researching, writing letters, and doing a lot of his firm's administrative work. But he has also had experiences that escape most large-firm associates. He has tried twelve cases in five years and had the chance to work pro bono at the public defender's office. And while it's certainly expensive to run a law firm, Jonathan now gets to take home the profits instead of handing them over to large-firm partners. "I have enough money to take Fridays off in the summers and go camping," Jonathan says. "And most importantly, my son is able to get all of the therapy he needs regardless of what is or isn't covered by insurance."

Speaking of insurance, Jonathan doesn't regret his start. "Your first job teaches you skills, like how to solve problems, which you can use in your chosen career later." He recommends to other prospective career changers that they first research what they want to do, and then figure out ways to do it profitably. Jonathan's father recently passed away from a heart attack, but Jonathan will never forget the impact the man had on his career. "My dad was very successful financially, but he was also a good person," he says. "I feel that as a personal injury attorney, I'm in a much better position to carry on that legacy."

Valerie
From Stockbroker to Pajama Manufacturer

As a child, Valerie was a female version of *Family Ties'* Alex P. Keaton. At thirteen, she started investing in the stock market, entranced with how one could turn a dollar into two simply by choosing the right investments. While attending California Polytechnic State University in San Luis Obispo on scholarship, Valerie interned at a local Dean Witter office and began planning a career as a stockbroker. The market crash that followed in 1987 might have discouraged some young professionals, but not Valerie. "I thought it was an opportune time to break into the business," she says. "And so, much to my family's dismay, I quit school and moved to Los Angeles."

At her first firm, Valerie found herself in a bit over her head. "I was a nineteen-year-old girl in a male-dominated business, and I was told I'd landed the job because of my looks," Valerie says. "Back then, sexual harassment lawsuits were virtually nonexistent, and I was working in the boys' club." Valerie used sex to her advantage in building a clientele. She owned several racehorses in partnership with her parents, and she met many of her male clients at the race-track. "Many of the rich owners threw me a few dollars to trade stocks for them. Had I been male, this probably wouldn't have happened." It was an uphill battle getting people to take her seriously, and she spent countless hours prospecting by phone, but Valerie's natural investment savvy and hard work helped her hold on to clients for the long term. Gradually, she worked her way up in the financial services industry, spending several years as a broker and trader and several more at an investor relations firm.

Despite her seniority, though, Valerie saw her income potential wane. In late 2004, she was paid a below-industry salary and a semiannual bonus based on profitability. That year, her company enjoyed its most lucrative period in its thirty-year history, and Valerie expected a substantial bonus. "A few days before Christmas, we were informed that they were going to use the money to invest in plush Beverly Hills and New York City offices and that there would be no bonus for the employees," she said. Naturally, Valerie felt cheated, and decided she had to figure out a way to bring home the paycheck she deserved. She began looking into independent business opportunities. "I wanted a pair of those kids' pajamas with the feet built in, but no one made them for adults," she said. "After doing my own focus group with friends and family, I concluded that the idea would be a viable venture."

In becoming a pajama manufacturer, Valerie's challenges were twofold. First, she had to master the mechanics of producing clothing from the ground up. "I had to do extensive research into the textile industry, as I had no experience there. I basically just committed myself 110 percent to learning everything about textile manufacturing and marketing," she says. "In doing this, I found the Internet to be the most amazing tool imaginable. For example, I hired a manufacturer online through a website called Alibaba.com, which is similar to Google but for manufacturers. I used other websites to locate freelancers who built me a website and helped me create graphics."

Next, Valerie needed to scale the fledgling business appropriately. The new company was self-funded, and Valerie invested around $60K initially. "The majority of that money was spent on inventory from my first manufacturing run," she explains. She experienced success right away through a few smart strategies. "I put up a 'coming soon' website about six months before I had anything to sell and collected email addresses from those who visited the site. Also before I had product, I attended MAGIC, the largest and most prestigious fashion and apparel trade show. I showcased my prototypes and took advance orders."

Valerie's new business, the Big Feet Pajama Company (www .bigfeetpjs.com), was a million-dollar business by its second year. The company offers fun footed pajamas to kids and adult men and women of every shape and size. The pj's are available in shirting flannel, cotton knit, micropolar fleece, and wool cashmere, and celebrities pictured on the company website include Bill and Hillary Clinton, Eva Longoria, Whoopi Goldberg, and Taylor Swift. Thanks to footed pajamas, Valerie had reached her financial goals at the age of thirty-nine. "My income has increased about fourfold, and I don't have to answer to anyone," she says. In the financial world, she developed the skills, as well as the determination, to transition to a career with greater earning potential. "I know marketing and I know sales, and I adhere to the principle that failure is not an option."

One thing's for sure: Valerie's world is always changing. "My company is very seasonal. About eighty percent of our business is done in the fourth quarter (near the December holidays). During that time, I generally spend fourteen to seventeen hours a day, seven days a week, overseeing the operations," she says. "But in our off-season, I work just a few hours a day. This morning, for example, I took my baby and dog in to talk to my employees. I was there less than an hour and took the rest of the day off!"

To other would-be clothing manufacturers, Valerie advises, "Don't jump in the pool with both feet. Start small and test the waters, and do your homework. If it looks like it will work out, scale up from there."

Kirsten
From Local Journalist to Compliance Manager

As a teen, Kirsten, now thirty-four, was the type of student every college wanted to accept. An athlete with good grades who also participated in theater, choir, and the literary magazine, Kirsten did not disappoint when she arrived at Carleton College in Northfield, Minnesota. She prepared to graduate, magna cum laude, and was named to the competitive Chicago Business Fellows at the University of Chicago Booth School of Business, a program that allowed her to start her MBA between her junior and senior year of college.

The job Kirsten wanted most was with General Mills. Each year, the company hired six people into their Executive Development Program, but the year Kirsten finished school, General Mills only took one person and she was candidate number two. "I really had my heart set on that job," says Kirsten. "And at that time, I didn't understand the notion of perseverance. I realize now that I could have kept in touch with General Mills and reinterviewed for the job if I wanted it so badly."

However, around the same time, Kirsten was participating in her college's phonathon. She was telling an alum that she'd always wanted to write, and his advice was to forget about the corporate world, and go work in a Laundromat and be a writer instead. "I decided that if I was going to be poor, I might as well do it in my twenties," she says. "So I moved to Minneapolis and worked at Starbucks for a while, picking up writing gigs here and there."

A major writing break arrived in the form of an internship at *Minnesota Law & Politics* magazine. Here, Kirsten wrote book reviews, profiles, and articles about topics such as whether a lawyer's faith interfered with her work. She also worked for *Family Handyman* magazine, and while she enjoyed liaising with attractive male editors who were all former tradesmen, she was beginning to realize that the romantic life of a writer wasn't all it was cracked up to be. "The pay was low, the competition was tight," says Kirsten. "Granted, I was in Minneapolis, where there are fewer opportunities than in, let's say, New York, but I began to realize that writing success depends on your ability to promote yourself, and that writing all the time is exhausting!"

Nevertheless, Kirsten was ecstatic when she was hired full-time at City Pages, the online news and arts weekly of the Twin Cities.

She had been an avid reader since college and had great respect for the writers there. Alas, from the time she walked in the door on her first day, Kirsten knew the job wasn't for her. "Although I had the opportunity to learn journalism from people I liked, and I had free access to any event I could possibly want to attend—from opera performances to sporting events to comedy shows—the collective atmosphere of the publication was so depressing. There was no team spirit. Every week, the paper would come out with these amazing stories, and people would walk right past the writers without saying a word."

It was also clear that advancement would be painfully slow. Kirsten was surrounded by talented people, all of whom had a several-year head start on her, and even they seldom had opportunities to move up. Meanwhile, Kirsten's relationship with the man she'd married at age twenty-four had collapsed, and when she couldn't support herself on her City Pages salary, she was forced to take a second job as a proofreader. Kirsten started looking at other avenues where she could make more money using her writing talent. "I looked into PR and advertising jobs, but I understood there to be a lot of dues-paying in those fields. Truth be told, I felt stuck."

Kirsten was concerned about transitioning away from writing completely. "I'd just spent five years building my career, and the last thing I wanted to do was start all over again at the bottom of another field. And by then, the dot-com boom was in full swing. I felt like I was missing out." However, some chance networking with a college classmate resulted in a job offer to do online legal training in Boston, Kirsten's relocation city of choice. The company had formed in response to the government's passage of the Federal Sentencing Guidelines, which, in combination with new pieces of federal legislation such as Sarbanes-Oxley, meant that companies ran significant financial risks that might be mitigated if they could show they had effective training in place on legal and ethical topics.

Kirsten was attracted by the stability of this prospective new career, and the fact that business realities had primed the company for growth. She was able to leverage her background researching and writing for *Minnesota Law & Politics* to prove she was a good fit for this new role, and she received a comfortable bump in salary. By the time Kirsten had been at her new job for a year, she was making more than she and her former husband had made combined.

Kirsten made a permanent move into corporate ethics and compliance consulting. Her current company creates online courses that raise awareness about legal and ethical issues at work for clients such as Coca-Cola, BP, Ford, and Google. She has acquired in-depth knowledge of more than one hundred business problems that have legal implications—from financial fraud to sexual harassment to obscure government regulations in the automotive or pharmaceutical industries. She has become skilled in product design and development, and is an expert at finding creative ways to use her company's products to meet clients' business needs. In addition to being financially satisfied, Kirsten is personally fulfilled. "I love my job," she says. "Seeing the company grow has provided a terrific education regarding how the world works, and I've learned so much about human nature and business strategy from the founders, who are all really smart people."

Today, Kirsten is glad she made the leap when she did. "It's difficult to work so hard for something and then realize it's not for you, but at some point it's sunk costs. You have to cut your losses and move on." She suggests that career switchers who want to increase their earning potential "go into a field where there's already money. Things are a lot easier when your company can afford adequate resources." She adds: "Also think about the value of what you do. A lot of people want to make more money, but they don't stop to think why someone should pay them. Then, look for a place of employment where you will keep learning and growing so that you'll be well positioned for advancement."

Now that she has an alternative career to distract herself, Kirsten feels she has actually grown as a writer. "Lately, I've been doing some writing and speaking in the compliance and ethics field, and am working on revising my first novel!"

☞ Self-Reflection: Is Money Your Motivation?

- When you think of goals for your life, is making a lot of money at the top of the list?
- Have you been told that there just isn't any money in your field anymore?
- Does the foreseeable trajectory for your career make it impossible to meet your long-term financial goals?
- Has your salary hovered in the same range for three to five years?
- Do you work fifty-plus hours a week, but find that you're still struggling to make ends meet?
- Did you grow up accustomed to a certain lifestyle, and are finding that your job now just doesn't cut it?
- Are there many things that you want or need that you can't afford?
- Does your spouse's career mandate that you step up your efforts to support the family?
- Do you find yourself constantly in debt because you are spending much more than you earn?
- Does your current career fail to offer you a means to save for your future, especially retirement?

👍 If you answered "Yes" to two or more of these questions, you may be primed to increase your income dramatically with a new career. Use the guidance in the next section to get moving.

☞ Putting the Change to Work

Adjust your thinking: "You cannot set a goal of a million dollars a year, make a career choice that pays $40K per year, and expect to be happy with your decisions and the money you make over time," says Susan Heathfield, the human resources guide for About.com. Also, if you're going to be successful in commanding a certain amount of money, you'll need to stop thinking of yourself as someone who isn't worth that much, because that attitude will be subtly—or not so subtly—communicated to those who are assessing how much to pay you.

Get out of debt: If you're carrying a great deal of debt, it's hard to get ahead financially in any career. According to J. D. Roth of the popular Get Rich Slowly blog, debt elimination involves three steps. The first is to stop acquiring new debt—don't finance anything, cut up your credit cards, and halt any recurring payments such as a gym membership or an online gaming account. The next step is to establish an emergency fund. Roth says that this should encompass approximately a thousand dollars in cash and be used for coping with unexpected expenses. The money should be kept liquid but not immediately accessible, via a savings account at an online bank such as ING. Finally, eliminate your existing debt by implementing a debt snowball. What does snow have to do with it? Here's the formula:

- Order your debts from lowest balance to highest balance.
- Designate a certain amount of money to pay toward debts each month.
- Pay the minimum payment on all debts except for the one with the lowest balance.
- Throw every other penny at the debt with the lowest balance.
- When that debt is gone, do not alter the monthly amount used to pay debts, but throw all you can at the debt with the next-lowest balance.

You should also call each financial institution you have debt with and try to negotiate a lower interest rate—ideally 5 to 12 percent. They will often oblige because they don't want you going to their competition. Once you're out of debt, save! Industry experts recommend setting aside 10–15 percent of gross income, or the equivalent of one hour's worth of income every day.

Choose a lucrative field: According to PayScale (www.payscale .com), career expert Laurence Shatkin analyzed current U.S. Labor Department figures and deemed the top-paying industries as information technology, finance, health care, and energy. Software developers, for example, command an annual median salary of $72.3K, physician assistants make an average of $63.5K, those in securities and commodity exchange make an average of $58.7K, and aerospace manufacturers make an average of $55K. Keep in mind that most senior-level employees in these positions earn well above the median. Sales can still be one of the most profitable careers out there, but as Wes Moss says in his book *Make More, Worry Less*, not all sales jobs are created equal. Look for a position where your sales quota doesn't reset to zero every year, where your commission is a reasonable percentage of each sale, and where you'll have the opportunity to run a sales team and get credit from those working beneath you. According to Moss, good sales jobs also allow for repeatable revenue, meaning that sales are generated through word of mouth with no extra effort on the part of the salesperson, and reoccurring revenue, meaning that income automatically comes in when a customer renews.

Given the current trend to ship jobs overseas, it's also a smart idea to look for careers that can't be outsourced. No matter where you live, the local population will be in need of hairdressers, plumbers, mechanics, and electricians.

You can use salary calculators on websites such as Salary.com and PayScale to determine your income potential in various fields, and the U.S. Bureau of Labor Statistics' website (www.bls.gov) is a great resource for comparing the salaries for specific jobs according to level and geographic location.

Choose a profitable company: If your career change will involve working at a company, be sure to select one with a high profitability ratio. In a nutshell, companies with high profitability ratios take in more income per unit sold than businesses with lower ratios. Businesses that have stayed profitable over the long term will continue to make money even in unfavorable conditions because they know how to limit costs and maximize profit potential. Is the company public? Monitor its stock price, forecasts, executive turnover, and paperwork submitted to the Securities and Exchange Commission. You can also do a Google search for recent financial news, and read the releases on the company's investor relations website. Additionally, in considering whether a particular organization will allow for rapid income growth, consider whether it has profit-sharing and stock purchase plans for employees, whether you would be eligible for performance bonuses, and whether the company will match your contributions to your retirement fund. Don't jump into a start-up situation without a healthy knowledge of the company's business plans and the market demand for its products or services.

Consider relocation: There's no doubt about it—if you want to live in New York City or San Francisco, you're going to need a lot of money. Your income will stretch a lot further in less expensive cities such as Atlanta or Dallas, where monthly rent for a one-bedroom apartment costs around $750. If you have your heart set on the Big Apple, however, you might at least think about selling your swanky condo and moving into a more affordable living space.

Improve your literacy skills: According to Steve Kaufmann of LingQ, a company that provides Web-based language tutoring, the most accurate predictor of earning power is literacy. Literacy is not just being able to read, it also refers to your command of written language. Kaufmann suggests copying a sample page from a source or article that interests you and pasting it into Google Documents. You can find several readability indicators under File/Word Count, including the Automated Reader Index, which indicates the number of years of schooling required to understand a text. Keep challenging yourself with harder and harder material until you are comfortable with content that is at an index of 12 or 15 or higher. You should also measure the richness of your vocabulary. Cut and paste a sample article into a Web-based vocabulary profiler such as the one at www.lextutor.ca/vp/eng. Using this kind of tool, you can see how many of the piece's words are within the one thousand most frequently used words, how many are "academic" (AWL), and how many are "off-list." Kaufmann recommends getting to the point where you are comfortable reading material that has 10 percent or more words in the AWL and the off-list categories. Don't forget that you can use online dictionaries and word learning programs to increase your vocabulary. When you come across a word that you don't know, get into the habit of looking it up immediately.

Go for that degree: If you checked out the Learning chapter, you read that U.S. census records indicate that lifetime income increases with degrees. Back to College and the College Board cite the gap in earning potential between a high school graduate and a bachelor's or master's degree holder as over $1 million. And there's a reason people borrow boatloads of money to obtain advanced degrees. Master's degree recipients may earn up to $2.5 million in their lifetime, and professional degree holders—in fields such as law and medicine—can make up to $4.4 million. Review chapter three for more advice on going back to school.

Hire a financial adviser: Financial planners can help you manage your money and plan for your financial future in the most effective way, often at little or no cost to you. The best way to select a planner is through word of mouth—just make sure you have similar needs as the person giving you the referral. You can also check out the Financial Planning Association (www.fpanet.org) to search for advisers by specialty or geography, and then verify their credentials with the Certified Financial Planner Board of Standards (www.cfp .net). Once you've pinpointed a few qualified professionals, interview each in person to get a comprehensive grasp of their services and to see if they're personally compatible with you. Also, make sure you understand how the planners get paid. Commission-based planners are paid by the companies whose products they sell, while fee-based planners may receive commission on some products they sell, but most of their income comes from a fee paid by you or a parent financial institution such as Citibank or JPMorgan Chase. Both types can be valuable, but be on the lookout for a planner who seems biased in favor of a particular product or family of products. Good planners should make an effort to get to know you in these meetings, probing for information about your financial history, current portfolio, investment philosophy, and tolerance for risk. Before you hire, talk with at least one current client reference. Ask how the adviser has performed over a period of time and how she handles challenging financial circumstances.

Start a side business: If you think the best path to a higher income is to launch a full-time entrepreneurial venture, chapter two provides inspirational stories, guidance, and resources for doing so. But it's also possible to make extra money moonlighting, or working at another job, while still gainfully employed. As long as you continue to do your day job well and refrain from using company resources for your new project, moonlighting can be a wonderful way to test-drive a new career while saving money for your transition. I have one friend who parlayed her hobby of making soaps into a profitable wholesale aromatherapy business, and another who made so much money offering college counseling to high school students via social networking that he eventually left his corporate job. Online sales outlets such as eBay and content outlets such as niche blogs have made becoming a part-time solopreneur easier and more affordable than ever. It's certainly one way to do what you love and keep additional funds coming in while you contemplate and plan for a full-blown career change. Relatively little risk and high reward!

☞ Exercise: Increasing Your Income

- Examine your current financial situation—your cash flow, assets, and liabilities—either on your own or with the help of a financial adviser. Brainstorm three ideas for weathering a transition where you have little or no income, including how much you will need to save before you can quit your job and how to curb unessential expenses.

- Write down three industries you're interested in working in that also have high income potential.

- Identify two successful people in each industry you selected. Over lunch or coffee, ask these individuals about their career trajectories and what they think are the important considerations for financial health in those fields. Write your key learnings here.

- Write three action steps to take this year with the eventual goal of doubling your income.

☞ Resource Toolkit

Websites

Economic Research Institute: www.erieri.com
Financial Planning Association: www.fpanet.org
Get Rich Slowly: www.getrichslowly.org
I Will Teach You to Be Rich: www.iwillteachyoutoberich.com
National Association of Personal Financial Advisors: www.napfa.org
PayScale: www.payscale.com
U.S. Bureau of Labor Statistics: www.bls.gov
Vocabulary.com: www.vocabulary.com

Books

Make Money, Not Excuses: Wake Up, Take Charge, and Overcome Your Financial Fears Forever (Jean Chatzky)
Secrets of the Millionaire Mind (T. Harv Eker)
Think and Grow Rich (Napoleon Hill)
Get Rich, Stay Rich, Pass It On: The Wealth-Accumulation Secrets of America's Richest Families (Catherine McBreen and George Walper, Jr.)
Make More, Worry Less, Secrets from 18 Extraordinary People Who Created a Better Income and a Better Life (Wes Moss)
The Wall Street Journal Complete Personal Finance Guidebook (Jeff Opdyke)
Women and Money: Owning the Power to Control Your Destiny (Suze Orman)
The Total Money Makeover: A Proven Plan for Financial Fitness (Dave Ramsey)

Passion

Anyone can dabble, but once you've made that commitment,
your blood has that particular thing in it,
and it's very hard for people to stop you.
—**Bill Cosby, comedian**

When I was in high school, I loved to act. I tried out for all of the
dramas and musicals and spent every day after classes rehearsing in
the cavernous theater. Nothing could compare to the rush I'd experience standing in the wings, preparing to make my first entrance,
or bowing to loud applause during the curtain call. Back then, I had
passion for acting with a capital *P*, and if I wasn't allowed to do it,
I thought I would die.

If you're reading this chapter, perhaps you have similar memories and you're gunning to turn your career in the direction of a passion you've had since childhood. However, after talking to several
people who were driven by passion, I don't necessarily believe it's
something you either have or you don't. Most of us, in fact, aren't
born with a particular passion. It's created over time based on what
excites our senses, what infuses us with energy, and what incites
us to achieve. There's no shame in admitting that you don't know
exactly what your passion is and wanting to take steps to find out.

Uncovering a latent passion can be just the catalyst you need to
launch a fulfilling career. You wouldn't be alone, for a recent Intuit
study found that 70 percent of small business owners were motivated to start their own businesses because of personal passion, and
believed that same passion assisted them in getting through economic downturns. In another report, *Money* magazine and Salary
.com surveyed thousands of career changers who all claimed passion
as a top priority. "Passion is the new king," says Meredith Hanra-

han, chief marketing officer at Salary.com. "It isn't about advancing to the next level. Most people in their second acts want their contributions to matter; they want a passion payoff. It's not optional; it's the new requirement."

People who act from passion are more successful because they experience life more fully in the present moment and write their own scripts as opposed to reading others'. Instead of watching the clock, they lose themselves in what they're doing and the workday seems to fly. They accomplish more in a shorter period of time, they challenge limitations, and they feel better about themselves. They're also physically healthier.

Whether you have an existing passion you wish to transform into a job, or you know you have one deep within you that you have yet to define, I hope the anecdotes and guidance in this chapter will set you on your way.

Jason
From Construction Worker to Photographer

Thirty-two-year-old Jason had a camera in his hand from a young age. "I had a cheap, plastic film one," he remembers. "Sometimes I took pictures with it and my mom would get them developed for me, and other times I would walk around with the camera pretending to take pictures even though there was no film in it. Some kids play cops and robbers and some play photographer."

Nevertheless, when Jason graduated from high school, it was assumed that he would enter the family trade of commercial construction. "My grandfather, father, uncles, and brother worked and still work in construction," says Jason. "I started as an apprentice hanging Sheetrock on residential sites, and shortly after my dad introduced me to commercial steel framing." He went on to master drywall, acoustic grid ceilings, and finishing—working on several large jobs around the Eugene, Oregon, area, including Autzen Stadium, the University of Oregon's Lillis Building, the *Register-Guard* building, and Lane Community College.

During his nine years in commercial construction, Jason learned to work with people as well as with his hands. "You have to know how to supervise workers and how to be supervised," he says. "I often had to improvise on my feet. When problems arose, I usually didn't have time to wait for someone else to figure it out. I just had to take care of the situation in the moment."

You wouldn't think of construction as a cutthroat career, but apparently it is. "It tested my character," Jason relates. "I had to contend with false accusations and the competitive nature of my co-workers and supervisors trying to get ahead." Over the years, Jason struggled to prove himself to the company owners and his colleagues by demonstrating that he was honest, dependable, and trustworthy. It exhausted him, and eventually he began to feel that he was reaching a dead end. "There was nothing more to learn, nowhere to go, and too many older workers being crippled from the wear and tear on their bodies."

Jason's mind wandered to his old passion of photography. He longed to do something that was more than just a job, something that would satisfy his hunger for artistic expression. "I love photography because it makes an impact so much greater than words. For example, it's difficult to describe a person your wife has not met before, but if you show her a good picture, it's much easier," Jason says. "Or, if you go on a trip to another country and afterward you're telling your stories, people will get a lot more out of them if you have photos to share."

Although he wasn't sure that he could pursue photography as a career, Jason purchased a Canon 20D SLR digital camera and began to play around with it. His wife, Amy, a graphic designer, saw potential in his work and encouraged him to get formal training. A talented local photographer, David Loveall, offered to give Jason private lessons. David, who had been in the business for more than thirty years and had worked as a photographer for the Navy SEALs and the *Los Angeles Times*, became Jason's mentor. "David's a genius with light and the technical aspects of photography," says Jason. "He taught me as much as I wanted to learn, allowing me to tag along on his jobs and providing me studio space. He has an excellent reputation and I was blessed to connect with him."

Although Jason had David to lean on, he was plagued by misgivings. "I constantly asked myself, 'Do I really have this gift?' Professional photography can be a rewarding career if it works out, but it's a risky business." And, as other people who follow their passion can attest, it's a process that often costs a lot of time and money. "Camera gear is very expensive," Jason says. "I've already invested twenty thousand dollars, and I'm still not done. I've also put in a lot of time learning when I could have been collecting a paycheck."

Of course, it's also challenging to land at the bottom of a new field and work your way up. "In construction, I toiled for years to build my reputation, and I had the added benefit of my father and brother's good status in the community. Here, I've had to start over and do things on my own," Jason says. Through it all, he has become committed and humble. "I realized that you can have all the talent in the world, but you still have to be willing to get your hands dirty and be disciplined and eager to grow. It's dangerous to think you have it all figured out."

Today, Jason couldn't be happier that he had the courage to step away from the family business and seek out work that is personally meaningful to him. "My job is very rewarding, and I love it," he says. "The best part is the role I have in making memories that people will have forever. When a wedding is over, what will stand the test of time is not the cake, the flowers, or the food. The photos will be around for generations to come, and that's very powerful."

"Photography is not always as glamorous as people make it out to be, but then again, sometimes it is," Jason adds. "It's similar to construction in that it's a hands-on work environment, and much more goes into it than simply grabbing a camera and taking a picture. There are aspects of the job that I don't enjoy as much as others, but when those things come up, I always think, at least it's not Sheetrock!"

Jason's new career at the helm of Jason Miller Photography (www.jasonmillerphotography.com) means he's always on the go. "If I have a scheduled shoot, I'll either stop off at the studio to pick up my gear and then head to the location, or I'll set up at the studio for whatever the job requires. Sometimes things change when the client shows up, and I'll have to think on my feet and turn my creative switch on and off," Jason explains. "People look to me for direction, to be the leader, and that means I have to do whatever it takes to be direct, efficient, and productive, and to always uphold my standard of quality."

Jason tells those who have identified a passion to assess how important it is to turn that passion into a career. "You have to look at the cost and see if it's worth it to you. If it is, don't stop and never give up unless it sacrifices your integrity or relationships with the people you love. And remember that even if you love what you do, your work should never define who you are."

Kate
From Sports Marketer to Nonprofit Administrator

Twenty-nine-year-old Kate was just six when her mother was diagnosed with breast cancer. At such a young age, she thought cancer was a bad word that started with a *k*, and she didn't understand the severity of the situation. "My family was very protective of my brother and me, and as a result, shared little information about the status of our mother's health," Kate remembers. One late April morning, she was in social studies class when the phone call came that her mother's life was over. "Numbed by the loss, I turned in one direction, my brother in another direction, and my father in another. Not because of the absence of love, but because of the presence of sadness and grief and guilt."

Kate surrounded herself with friends and activities—everything from basketball and band to school and community clubs. Upon graduating from high school, she attended the University of Virginia in Charlottesville. During her senior year, Kate took an internship with the athletic department's marketing and promotions group, which in turn led to her first job in sports marketing with the Chick-fil-A Peach Bowl, a college bowl game held in Atlanta. "I chose sports because of the happiness that it brings to other people," Kate explains. "Walk into any sporting arena and you see so many smiles, hear so many cheers. People want to be there. It's an amazing moment in time, and I was driven by the fact that I could be a part of it."

Kate followed the Peach Bowl with a position at a sports and entertainment marketing agency. She led the team responsible for managing a global client's sponsorship with NASCAR. "Here I took on a more strategic role. I was able to exhibit my ambitious, creative side by developing customer and employee marketing programs for the client," she says. But although she was good at her job, something was missing for Kate. As a teenager, she'd been involved with a bereavement camp in Virginia. "While a counselor at the camp, I was able to see and feel the benefit of bringing young people together who had shared the experience of loss. I became aware of this vital element of support that I did not have as a child, and the need to bring it to kids during the most influential time of their lives."

As Kate considered her past and the personal journey she'd been through as a result of her mother's death, she dreamed of starting an organization for bereaved children. Slowly, her vision took shape in the form of Kate's Club (www.katesclub.org), a nonprofit with the goal of empowering children who are grieving the loss of a loved one. "I wanted to use my passion to build a program for children to find fun, friendship, support, and healing," says Kate. Even working in professional sports, she had always carried a mission of connecting the community through positive, uplifting experiences, and Kate's Club was no exception. Her transition to the new career, she says, was big and quick. Kate started with just six children and their families and an outing to a local bowling alley, and with the full support of her friends and family, has now been able to touch the lives of more than 170 children—creating a staff of 100 volunteers and a vibrant curriculum of social, emotional, and recreational programs.

As founder of the organization, Kate maintains that she has the best job. "I get to share Kate's Club and the important work we do with the world. I like to think of myself as an ambassador for these children, who, unfortunately, are often not given a voice in our culture." Her daily life includes fund-raising meetings, media calls, and outreach initiatives to ensure that Kate's Club operates in the most beneficial, efficient way, and as a direct result of her efforts, it continues to grow and thrive.

Most twenty-somethings who aim to start nonprofit organizations mean well but end up failing. What sets Kate apart? "My generation was brought up with the privilege of continued education, and I have a lot of peers who were paralyzed by the amount of opportunity in the workforce when they first left college or graduate school," she relates. "As I was seeking direction in my early twenties, my dad told me to make this decade about learning and experiences, not about money." This, along with the advice that trying and failing yields less regret than never trying at all, shaped Kate's professional trajectory.

Kate also cites her social skills as essential to her success. "Networking plays such a big part in any business, private or public sector. My contacts in the sports world were the core reason that Kate's Club was able to get off the ground. Their support helped me organize the first programs, which, not surprisingly, were held at sports events and venues." The most important factor of all, though, was Kate's love for what she was doing and a strong inner desire to make it work. "I knew in my twelve-year-old soul that the world needed Kate's Club."

Although she arrived at her career change from a unique angle, Kate believes that it's possible for anyone to fulfill their passion through a professional endeavor. "I think that the fundamentals of making a career change can be found in three *P*'s—patience, or taking each day one step at a time; purpose, or seeing the change as part of a professional evolution; and passion, or having the drive to get through long hours and seemingly insurmountable challenges," she says. Kate feels lucky to have had all three, and to be in a position to lead and inspire families all over the country. "People don't think that a topic like grief can bring joy to people's lives, but it can, and I wouldn't have my career any other way."

Gerry
From Minister to Publicist

Hailing from Boston, Gerry studied architecture, philosophy, and religion with enthusiasm before graduating cum laude from Birmingham-Southern College in Alabama. Unsure of whether he wanted to be a professor of religion or an ordained minister, Gerry decided to pursue a master's program that would allow him maximum flexibility in terms of career options. "I chose Harvard Divinity

School, and while there I completed several internships in a church, a soup kitchen, and a hospital," says Gerry. "Those positive experiences, combined with a disillusionment with my professors' lifestyles, slowly but surely pushed me in the direction of ministry."

In his second year of study, Gerry began the ordination process of the United Methodist Church (UMC), which included enrolling in certain classes and taking a battery of tests. At his graduation at the age of twenty-five, he became a deacon and was assigned to Bethany UMC in Sylacauga, Alabama. "This was an odd choice for me since I had always lived in cities and suburbs and hadn't been a regular churchgoer in my youth," says Gerry. "I'd wanted to be an associate pastor at a large church so that I could learn from a day-to-day mentor and stay within my demographic comfort zone. Instead, I was assigned as the sole pastor of a small church in rural Alabama. From the front door of my church and my parsonage, the only neighbors I could see were cows."

Still, Gerry jokes that he learned more about ministry in three months at Bethany UMC than he did in three years at Harvard. An intellectual and analytical person, Gerry found that his people skills were of utmost importance. He became an integral part of the community, serving as a substitute teacher for the local schools, refereeing basketball and softball games, and helping one of his parishioners clean chimneys. As church membership grew as a result of Gerry's involvement, he found himself testing traditional boundaries. "I published an article in defense of the acceptance of homosexuality—which went over like a lead balloon—and supported the establishment of a halfway house for rehabilitated ex-convicts."

Church leaders selected Gerry to attend the Academy for Congregational Development, a yearlong series of seminars and conferences focused on marketing the church. It was here that he realized he had a passion for marketing and immediately began to apply what he learned to his day-to-day church life. Once he was fully ordained as an elder in the UMC, Gerry moved to Faith UMC near Birmingham. Once again he was able to use his communication skills to get the church moving in a more positive direction. By then, however, Gerry had gotten married, and his wife needed to return to New England. He took a new position in the Bryantville UMC in Pembroke, Massachusetts. "This church had been through a lot of traumas, including high-profile deaths and accusations of sexual misconduct, and even though I poured my heart and soul into it, I couldn't fix it," he laments.

As a sense of futility set in, Gerry began to question his career choice. "From the beginning of my ministry, I'd felt like a square peg in a round hole. Not having grown up in the church, the trappings of ministry were an uncomfortable fit. I found myself wondering, 'What if I misheard my calling? What would I do if I wasn't doing this?' But in my first two churches, my results were lauded, and when everyone is patting you on the back and telling you how wonderful you are, it's easy to push back the doubts."

After seeing a counselor, Gerry realized that the aspect of the ministry he cared most about was marketing. He took a college course and was especially intrigued by public relations. "I'd followed my heart into the ministry, and now it was time to follow it out," he says. But Gerry was in for a difficult transition. "First, I wrestled with the question of whether I was turning my back on God, and eventually found solace in the Bible story of Jonah, which described a man who was called to a ministry that was limited in scope and time." Another obstacle was Gerry's mother, who vocally opposed his decision to leave the ministry. "Though I have forgiven her, I doubt I will ever forget how hard she made things for me," Gerry says.

But as one might expect, Gerry's biggest challenge was convincing commercial public relations agencies to hire an ex-minister. "With some creative spinning of the relevant skills from the ministry, I was able secure interviews with a few Boston-based agencies." He quickly learned the difference between agencies that were able to see how the skill set of a minister could benefit their clients, and agencies who called because of the novelty of an ex-minister looking for a job in PR. Gerry's big break finally came when he met a marketing director for GTE Internetworking at a job fair. The man was impressed with Gerry's story and recommended him to his PR firm, FitzGerald Communications. Gerry was called for an interview a few days later and got the job.

Now a youthful thirty-something, Gerry rose to the rank of manager at FitzGerald and eventually to the position of senior managing director at RF|Binder Partners. He represents organizations focused on health care in the developing world and government agencies in emerging markets that are seeking foreign investment from the United States. "I work with ambassadors, executives, and officials from India, Europe, Africa, and South America, manage teams of people across the country, and speak with media that can influence the people I need to influence and spread the messages I need to spread," Gerry says. "In this new career, I found what I should have received in the ministry—a sense that I am improving the world in some small way. The business world has given me a sense of purpose that I never had before."

Gerry experienced a lot of rejection in his months of job searching, but he proved far more resilient and adaptable than he imagined. "I channeled negative feelings into an effort to present myself more effectively to the world—turning every interaction into an opportunity and learning from everyone I met," he says. "I also never wasted time. If I went on an interview that was going nowhere, I made sure I didn't leave without suggestions for how to improve."

Gerry advises other passion seekers to proceed even if they're afraid. "There were many points where I could have taken the easy way out. I could have stayed in the ministry for fear of disappointing my mother or God. I didn't allow those fears to control me. I faced them, worked through them, and went on to find greater fulfillment and happiness," he says. "You should also determine your ultimate goal in life. Mine, for instance, is to leave the world a better place than I found it. Over the years in my new career, I have used experiences, education, and advocacy to do just that."

Tara
From Behavior Therapist to HIV Counselor to Doula

Tara's career journey started when she left college in Washington, D.C., and got married at the age of twenty-two. She had hoped to relocate to New York City, but her husband received an offer that moved the family to Philadelphia. Tara fell into a job as an early-intervention therapist for autistic toddlers. "I really hated it and had a hard time admitting this," she says. "Imagine the faces of people when you tell them 'I work with autistic kids—and I hate it.' The second part never escaped my lips, but I left that job after a year."

Tara enjoyed her second position as an HIV counselor at the Mazzoni Center a lot more. She had a wonderful boss who mentored her and took the time to probe about Tara's passion for women's health. "Instead of sending me out to work with male drug users, she put me on a project with pregnant women who were at high risk for HIV." Over the next few years, Tara learned a great deal, including how to run a business, how to counsel people, and how to manage delicate political situations. But she wanted more. "I had a few HIV-positive pregnant women who didn't have partners and were preparing to have their babies in the hospital on their own. Even as a young woman I knew instinctually that these women needed someone to be with them, holding their hands, while they were birthing their children. I felt that I should join them, so I did."

In her newly created role, Tara was shocked at what she witnessed. HIV-positive mothers-to-be were often talked down to or ignored by the doctors and nurses. "These women had no confidence in their bodies or the birthing process, which discouraged me. But on the other hand, I was so exhilarated when the babies were born." At this point, Tara was twenty-five and desperate to get out of her marriage. She lamented the fact that no one had talked her out of it in the first place, and the fact that she was sacrificing her dream of living in Manhattan.

In a last-ditch effort to save their relationship, Tara's husband gave in to her grievances and the couple moved to New York. There Tara learned that what she had been doing in the delivery room had a name—doula. Tara could get certified, meet other doulas, and build a business around her services. "I started begging pregnant women on the street to let me come to their births, and some of them took me up on the offer," she says. Just as things seemed to be taking off, though, Tara's mother was diagnosed with cancer. "I decided to drive from New York City to Princeton, New Jersey, three days a week to help my stepfather take my mother to and from radiation and chemo. After all, my stepdad still had to pay the bills while I was the one trying to build a business that no one understood."

For eight months, Tara was by her mother's side as the older woman fought a losing battle. During her trips to the hospital, Tara dreamed of attending births and thought about how much she hated her husband. "My body changed because of the stress, but somehow I kept going," Tara says. "And then, one day in chemo, my mom introduced me to a friend she had made. She placed her hand on my knee and said, 'This is my daughter Tara. She lives in New York and is Happily Married.' I couldn't believe that my own mother didn't know how miserable I was. It literally made me sick to my stomach. I knew that things had to change—and soon."

When Tara's mother passed away, she immediately revisited her goal of becoming a doula. "Almost everyone I knew told me that I'd have to get a real job, which infuriated me. Why couldn't they see that I was doing what I was meant to be doing? My stepfather, who had his own business as a book jacket designer, was the only person who said that of course I had to keep the doula business. He assured me I would fail, and that I would also keep going." It was a few years before Tara no longer had to worry about where she'd find her next client, and for a time it was a full-time job figuring out how to get a loan and work space. There were times when she despaired that she wouldn't make her rent, all the while struggling to build a reputation in the doula community. "A lot of the doulas I met had been doing things the same way for a long time, and it was hard when people I admired didn't support me. But I fought to stay true to myself, and I learned that I have a passion for business strategy sizzling inside me."

Today, Tara heads up two companies: the national Gifted at Birth (www.giftedatbirth.com) and the New York City–based Power of Birth (www.powerofbirth.com). She works from home for the first half of the day, and then heads into her Manhattan office around noon. In addition to attending around five births a month, Tara schedules and holds meetings with clients in their homes, provides pregnancy counseling, teaches childbirth education classes, and speaks at evening events for moms-to-be and new moms. By believing that anything is possible if you stay focused and make connections, and by asking the right questions and staying responsive to her clients, Tara has transformed her longtime passion into a lucrative career and has advanced the doula cause in the process!

Tara tells other prospective career changers to map out their ideas. "Keep a journal with you at all times because an idea will pop into your head when you are not planning on it," she says. "Talk to people about your ideas and take their feedback in, but always go with your gut in the end." The approach continues to work for Tara as her career reaches greater heights. "I can't wait to find out what the next decade holds!"

Kristin
From Paralegal to Advertising Copywriter

At twenty-three, Kristin is one of the youngest people to be profiled in this book. Not too long ago, she was destined to become a lawyer. But Kristin was lucky to pinpoint her passion early, and now she's on a trajectory she's certain is the perfect one.

When Kristin graduated from high school in 2003, she was interested in law and politics, and at McDaniel College in Westminster, Maryland, she majored in political science and international studies. "By the end of my sophomore year, I realized how much I missed my writing hobby, and added on a minor," she says. "I graduated in 2007 and had already been accepted to Villanova Law School. I was supposed to start that fall, but I decided to follow my sister's path. Because law school is so time-consuming and such a major fiscal responsibility, she'd worked as a paralegal before deciding that law school was right for her."

Kristin scored a job as a paralegal at a small law firm, an easy process given her extensive pre-law background. "Not only was I a political science major, but I was also in Phi Alpha Delta, an international law fraternity, and the Maryland Student Legislature. Both of these allowed me to do mock trials and legal research." Kristin was enthusiastic about her paralegal position. "I was prepared to surround myself with law practices. I'd have an advantage over other students when I got to law school and would receive a salary in the meantime," she says.

Kristin was soon ensconced in the daily life of a paralegal, which involved dissecting legal research, interviewing potential and existing clients, and working with the executive partners to discuss interview notes. But the longer Kristin worked, the more it occurred to her that while she was interested in law, she couldn't see doing it as a career. "Each day I felt more and more deflated. I missed the freedom of writing. Since I was little, I'd written poetry and other creative pieces—typically revolving around harder times in my life, such as my father's cancer. But any writing you do in law is static and flat," she says. "Eventually, I had such a bad taste in my mouth that I decided to seek a job at a creative agency where I could reap the joys of writing with fewer limitations."

Although it may have been a smart decision to get out of the profession before she'd invested a great deal of time and money on law school, Kristin found the transition challenging. "I was geared up for a world of structure—doing things in black and white and in order. It was tough to convince myself that my career didn't have to relate directly to my educational focuses on political science and law. It was more of a mental roadblock than anything," she says.

Kristin got to work retooling her résumé, using the writing experience generated by her college minor to get in the door with creative agencies. "I found that I was able to use the people skills I'd developed from my paralegal days to make the best impression while interviewing," she says. Within a relatively short period of time, Kristin landed a job at Singularity Design in Philadelphia, an agency that uses the Web medium to forge an emotional connection between a brand and its consumers.

Going from working in a conservative law firm to working in a laid-back creative agency was a 180-degree shift for Kristin, but she took to her new environment "like a fish to water." She did, however, have to work on opening up during meetings because her conservative law firm had taught her to keep many of her thoughts to herself. Today Kristin spends her days brainstorming witty headlines and writing ads. "I do all of the writing for my company, and the tasks vary. For example, when working on copy for a client or for internal purposes, a week or two will be focused on doing research to achieve the correct tone." One of Kristin's recent achievements was rebranding her agency and writing all of the copy for the new website at www.singularitydesign.com.

Kristin believes she has found the career she'll have for life, but if not, she now has the confidence to go after work she feels passionate about. "I know so many people who settle for jobs they hate rather than follow their dreams. Yes, changing careers is hard, and a lot of people aren't willing to go through the struggle that it requires," she says. "I had to fight for what I wanted for a bit, but it was worth it. I was seeing too much negativity bubbling up into other areas of my life—like my personal relationships—and I knew it was time." In trying to find the work you're meant to do, Kristin advises, listen to your head, but let your heart in on the action, too. "You'll find that a blend of the two creates a balance of what's practical and what you really want."

☞ Self-Reflection: Is Passion Your Motivation?

- Throughout your life, have you been disappointed when a particular activity ended because you wished it would last forever?
- Are there commonalities that unite all of the extracurricular endeavors in which you take part (for example, a love of community, a desire to learn)?
- Are you energized by one particular aspect of your work, but feel that you don't get to experience it enough?
- Do you have a cause you feel strongly about but you haven't pursued professionally because you fear you can't make it work?
- Do you find yourself working harder at your volunteer position than you do at your job?
- Has a unique personal experience led you to want to help others in the same situation?
- Is there a particular subject that you could talk about with enthusiasm all night, without ever getting tired?
- Have you harbored a secret dream for years that you haven't even shared with your close friends and family?
- Is there a group of books on your shelf devoted to a topic that's unrelated to your current job?

- Do you feel like you have no choice but to pursue your passion even if there are sacrifices involved?
- Does your heart typically influence your decision more than your head?

👍 If you answered "Yes" to two or more of these questions, passion might be a major motivator for you. Read on for ways that you can channel your emotion into a satisfying professional life.

☞ Putting the Change to Work

Consider passion's various faces: At the beginning of the passion exploration process, it's natural to feel a bit confused and overwhelmed. After all, *passion* is a vague term that is often thrown around, but in fact means different things to different people. I will tell you that I really enjoyed Richard Chang's book *The Passion Plan*. Chang, who presents a seven-step model for bringing greater passion into your personal and professional lives, describes passion as content-based (activities like writing, hosting events, or racing cars) or context-based (themes like innovation, nurturing, and risk taking). Chang says that we can experience both types of passion in our work and can often find ways to weave our passions into a current job without making a drastic career change. Indeed, in my speeches to would-be entrepreneurs, I often suggest that the passion for innovation be satisfied by joining an "intrapreneurship" committee that develops ideas for new products, services, and operations on behalf of the well-established organization.

Analyze what you bring to the table: According to Tom Siciliano and Jeff Caliguire, authors of *Shifting into Higher Gear: An Owner's Manual for Uniting Your Calling and Career*, defining your passion involves considering:

- What you do really well
- What makes you unique
- What moments in your past have proven the most memorable to you (examples: "I can still remember shouting with excitement when I was teaching my neighbor to ride her bike and she first

took off on her own" and "I recruited the kids on my block to open a lemonade stand—we made a ton of money!")

- What you have that the world needs

Every individual has a distinctive mix of physical traits, personality, gifts, skills, natural abilities, experiences, training, and interests, which means that only you can do the work you do in the exact way you do it. And when you accomplish something you're perfectly suited for, you feel alive and fulfilled, as if you're making the world a better place. Depending on your point of view, this might seem overly scientific or overly abstract. Remember that the point is to identify what you love doing, where your energy comes from, and why. Do not pass go and do not collect $200 without taking some real time with this one. You can get a jump start by completing the exercise in the next section.

Tune in to your spiritual life: At various points in my life, I've been a practicing Jew, an atheist, and an agnostic. But these days, I tend to believe that there is a higher power that guides our actions and decisions. The universe is not setting us up to fail, or to go through our lives without achieving anything of worth. Everything happens for a reason, there *is* a plan, and if we look carefully enough, we can unearth spiritual clues that will lead us to our true calling. Siciliano and Caliguire say that we can get closer to our passion core by paying attention to past occurrences in which we achieved success far beyond what we expected, and acknowledging the spiritual gifts that made such a high level of accomplishment possible. Over the course of my ten-year career, I've realized that my spiritual gifts are teaching, helping, and encouraging. Yours might include leading, evangelizing, giving, and administrating, among others.

Assess your values: Siciliano and Caliguire liken values to the foundation, walls, and roof of a house in the way they support, shape, and protect our lives. Core values (the foundation) include integrity, service, adventure, and generosity; family and relationship values (walls) include affection, quality time, community, and mentoring; career and work values (roof) include independence, competition, prestige, and financial security. Additionally, many of us have experienced intense hardships or disappointments, and a value that spans all three areas is to prevent others from suffering the same fate. This was the case with civil rights legend Martin Luther King, Jr., and Parkinson's disease advocate Michael J. Fox. It was also true for Kate, whose story you just read about. By gaining an understanding of your value set and what's truly important to you, not only will you learn more about your passion, but you will also be more capable of making smarter life choices.

Hold a passion party: Do you have a bunch of friends who are in the same boat? Gather them together over dinner and wine and discuss how you can integrate passion into an existing or new career. If they share your passion for a particular area, so much the better. Enthusiasm is contagious and you will play off one another. Follow the standard brainstorming rules—you are all blank slates, nothing is impossible, and there are no bad ideas. Prepare some thought-provoking questions in advance, such as "What does passion mean to us?," "What are our most defining characteristics?," and "What careers are most appealing based on these characteristics?" Assign one guest as the scribe and make sure everyone gets a copy of the notes after the event.

Unleash your creativity: Do you think that only kids and artists can be creative? We all have the ability, and sometimes being imaginative is the best way to come up with new ways to employ your passion. Commit a block of time in an environment that's conducive to productive thought, and clear your head. Make a conscious effort to stop thinking about all of your everyday concerns—such as the project you have due next week or the fight you had with your significant other—and engage in a creative activity. Play a game with a child, draw a picture, or work a puzzle. Turn on a favorite CD or iTunes mix or read a poem that resonates with you. Call one of your more artistic friends and ask what she does to get the juices flowing, and talk about how you might take your own sense of creativity to the next level.

Try your passion on for size: What interests do you have related to your passion, and what activities are available to you that you've never tried before? You should sample as many elements of your passion as you can, even if they're unorthodox or off the wall. For example, if you've developed a passion for caring for the elderly as a result of interacting with your ninety-one-year-old grandfather and you think you might pursue a career in nursing, visit a local assisted-living facility and spend some time talking to the residents and the staff. Follow that up by taking a continuing education course to see if you would really enjoy the daily work. Similarly, if you love to knit baby clothes for friends and family, you might try your hand at selling and promoting your work at the summer flea markets to see if the business side appeals to you. It is exactly this type of experimentation that will help you determine if your passion is better suited to a hobby or a new career.

Seek a passion mentor: Join third-party associations or networking groups composed of individuals who share your passion. You'd be surprised how many organizations are out there and the diversity of professions and initiatives they support. You might, for instance, be passionate about organization and delight in helping your friends rearrange their closets or basements. Just a few minutes of online research would uncover a chapter of the National Association of Professional Organizers (www.napo.net) in nearly every major city. Become an integral part of the group you join, attending events and developing relationships with those who are a few years ahead of you on the journey. Correspond regularly with promising and successful people who can show you the ropes and provide you with advice for transforming your love into a steady paycheck. Just don't forget to offer them something in return!

Volunteer for a cause: Volunteering allows you to try out a new and exciting field that you may not have enough experience to get a paid position in, and the opportunity to do work that aligns with your passion. It may also provide critical skills training so that you are better prepared for a future career change. In addition, donating your time allows you to test-drive a leadership role. Volunteer organizations need people to coordinate projects, and they usually aren't picky about your age or background. You may find yourself in a position to achieve more than you ever dreamed possible. Finally, research has demonstrated that a satisfying volunteer gig improves self-esteem, lowers blood pressure, and reduces the physical effects of stress on the body.

Pretend that getting a passion-oriented job is a school project: Imagine that you're being graded on how well you master the subject of your passion, and that you have to present to an instructor and class a realistic plan for creating a new career from it. Start by devising short- and long-term goals, timelines, and deadlines so that a paying job incorporating your passion becomes a definite outcome instead of a theoretical consideration. "You need to think about each step it will take to get there," says Curt Rosengren, passion expert and the author of the M.A.P. Maker blog. "That will determine how fast you can realistically move. Some people can make a single dramatic change, but most can't. It's critical to identify internal and external obstacles. If you can't change immediately, build the foundation over time with a dual track. Take consistent baby steps, and when the time comes to change, it will be closer to stepping off a curb than jumping off a cliff."

Manage existing responsibilities: Whether you're carrying a ton of student debt, you're already married with a family to support, or just coping with current economic realities, you may not be in a position to quit your day job and chase your dream unencumbered. "Money is the most common external roadblock," agrees Rosengren. "I've seen people circumvent it by saving money to take the edge off the financial challenges of a career change, and by pushing the ultimate goal temporarily onto the backburner. You can also look for short-term revenue streams to help bridge the gap." My friend Paul, for instance, was an administrative assistant by day and a student by night as he secured the necessary schooling to become a veterinarian. Another acquaintance bartered homemade meals for child care when she was forced to leave her two daughters to train as a cyclist. Chapters two and four provide additional suggestions for overcoming the financial hurdles associated with career change.

Ignore the naysayers: Whether you want to become a boutique owner or a television broadcaster, launching a career around your passion requires a leap of faith, and there will be those who have no problem telling you that you're crazy and should stick with the career you chose years ago and now make a good living doing. Difficult as it may be, you must stop worrying about what other people think, because, as the stories in this chapter have illustrated, you won't be able to please everyone all of the time. Make an effort to silence your own inner critic as well, because turning into the little engine that couldn't is a surefire way to kill your motivation and progress. Focus on doing what you know in your heart to be the right course of action, and don't look back.

Pull the plug on pressure: I'll close this section with a cautionary note about an issue I've faced in my own career. There have been times when I've become so obsessed with my new passion-based writing career and I've put so much pressure on myself to become well-known that I've lost the emotion that led me there in the first place. You never want to be in a situation where you feel like you don't have a choice and are constantly being forced to act, because next thing you know, you'll be shopping for a new passion. Make sure that your implementation plans leave breathing room and enough support to preserve your love of the game.

☞ Exercise: Identifying Your Passion

- Think back to when you were in third grade and were asked what you wanted to be when you grew up. What was your answer, and why?

- Who are your role models, and what is it that you admire about these people? Write down two qualities for each.

- For one day, put your world under a microscope. Write down four things that inspired or excited you—for example, a story on the news, a conversation at a dinner party, or an interaction you witnessed on the subway. What do your reactions tell you about yourself?

- Pretend for a moment that you're independently wealthy. What three jobs would you want to do if you weren't financially compensated?

- When you think of your dream job(s), what comes to mind? What are three things that appeal to you about this job or jobs, and if the job is probably unattainable (becoming a famous musician, for instance), are there other ways you could fulfill your passion for it?

- Spend a half hour sitting outside in your favorite park, or, if it's winter, in a quiet room in your house. Breathe deeply and let your mind wander. When you're fully relaxed, ask yourself what really makes you content in life. Write your preliminary thoughts here.

- Call a friend or relative and share what you've learned about your passion or purpose. Then make notes here on the "who," "where," and "how" components of your passion. Who do you want to work with, where do you want to work, and what type of work do you want to do?

- Research three potential careers that will satisfy all of these passion components, and write two action steps you'll take in the next month to learn more about each.

☞ **Resource Toolkit**

Websites
Creativity Portal: www.creativity-portal.com
Queendom: www.queendom.com
Quintessential Careers: www.quintcareers.com
Passion Catalyst: www.passioncatalyst.com
Pathfinders: www.pathfinderscareerdesign.com
Pursue the Passion: www.pursuethepassion.com
Steve Pavlina: www.stevepavlina.com
The One Question: www.theonequestion.com

Books
The Passion Plan (Richard Chang)
I Don't Know What I Want, But I Know It's Not This (Julie Jansen)
What Is Your Life's Work? (Bill Jensen)
Passion at Work (Lawler Kang)
What Color Is Your Parachute? (Richard Nelson Bolles)
Shifting into Higher Gear: An Owner's Manual for Uniting Your Calling and Career (Tom Siciliano and Jeff Caliguire)
The Creative Habit: Learn It and Use It for Life (Twyla Tharp)
Career Match: Connecting Who You Are with What You Love to Do (Shoya Zichy)

Setback

I do not accept that I have come to the end of the road.
When one door closes, another one opens.
—**David Sanders, author**

Some of the most memorable careers in history have been launched on the heels of a major setback. We've all heard their stories. Bestselling children's author J. K. Rowling supported herself as a secretary and wasn't able to devote herself to writing about Harry Potter until she was let go and received a severance package that allowed her to take some time off. Michael Bloomberg lost his job—and a bundle of money—when his firm Salomon Brothers was acquired by what is now Citigroup. But instead of opting for early retirement, Bloomberg went out on his own and founded a billion-dollar media empire, and then, years later, reinvented himself again as a political dynamo.

When you're forced to give up your job as a result of a pink slip, a medical diagnosis, or other unfortunate circumstances, it may seem as if your life will never get back on track. But the career changers I'll profile in this chapter show us that sometimes, setbacks can be blessings in disguise. At the time, you may think that the universe is working against you. It happened to me. In 2003, my promising fiction writing career stalled when my publisher went out of business a few months before my first book was released. Deeply discouraged, I accepted that I would never be a writer and went back, head hanging, to my day job in public relations.

It was tempting to think of myself as a victim and to lapse into prolonged negativity and depression. But once I allowed myself a little time to come to terms with my feelings, I focused on making a comeback. I shopped my finished book to new publishers and eventually sold it to an even stronger house.

In the following pages, you'll get to know individuals who took their own batches of lemons and, with a little perseverance and ingenuity, came out with the sweetest of all lemonades. Then, in case you're in the midst of coping with your own setback, I'll close with some tips for overcoming it and using it as a platform to succeed beyond your wildest dreams.

Patrick
From Electronic Sales Executive to Motivational Speaker

Thirty-eight-year-old Patrick dreamed of being a football hero all his life, and when he received a college football scholarship, he was one step closer to having his wish of playing in the NFL come true. But during his freshman year, Patrick suffered a back injury—in an instant ending a career that had taken years to cultivate. Disillusioned and heartbroken, Patrick bought a one-way bus ticket to Missoula, Montana. He figured he'd nurse his wounds by continuing his college education in a location that offered world-class mountain biking and skiing. When it came time for Patrick to decide what he wanted to do for a living, he naturally turned to sales. Growing up in Michigan, he'd been one of his neighborhood's top door-to-door salesmen of the *Detroit Free Press*. It made sense, and so after Patrick got married, he and his wife moved to Seattle, where Patrick took a job as a corporate travel sales executive.

At Avis Rent A Car, Patrick discovered that he could close major Fortune 500 accounts simply by beating the Hertz price by one dollar. This realization, combined with his natural likability and steel resolve in the face of rejection, led Patrick to become the number-one Avis salesperson in the country. "Early on, I learned that friends buy from friends, so gaining trust and establishing real relationships was a must," says Patrick. "Also, if someone was not interested, I just had to move on. As the saying goes, 'Some will, some won't, so what, someone else is waiting.'"

At twenty-seven, Patrick was courted by numerous corporate sales organizations. Taking a job at South Bay Circuits, he doubled his salary and moved seamlessly into the area of business-to-business electronics sales. With that experience, he was now even more marketable to the computer manufacturers that populated the Pacific Northwest during Silicon Valley's heyday. In particular, Patrick was pursued by one older gentleman who longed to take the young superstar under his wing. "This guy really turned into a mentor for me, and when he offered me a great package with stock that was rising by the minute, I had to jump on the opportunity," he says.

At Merix Corporation, a high-end circuit board manufacturer, Patrick became the worldwide account manager for Intel, and despite spending hours a day driving back and forth from Intel's operation in Oregon to his home outside of Seattle, he was happier and more successful than he'd ever been. He was pulling down a six-figure salary in a prestigious position, and he was barely thirty years old.

Then came September 11, 2001. Merix's stock plummeted, and a national trend of manufacturing outsourcing spelled trouble for the company. When the man who had been Patrick's mentor and father figure sat him down in a Starbucks and let him go, Patrick was devastated. "I still remember driving home on the freeway, betrayed and disgusted. I'd given this company my soul, and I'd done well for them. I loved sales, but I knew that I couldn't trust Corporate America anymore," he says. The months that followed were dark times in Patrick's life. He and his wife had to sell the house they'd built, and getting too far behind on bills left his family without utilities. "My wife and I had a 'come to Jesus' talk, and in the end I took another corporate job."

His heart wasn't in it. Patrick had decided that he wanted to become a motivational speaker, to share with others how his vision to succeed had fueled him all these years and how he'd overcome life's hurdles. Quietly, Patrick liquidated some of his remaining assets and, using his skills as a salesman, started marketing himself on the lecture circuit. He self-published a book with his messages, and speaking gigs at corporations, nonprofit organizations, and universities began coming in. Patrick felt the demands of his new business bumping up against the responsibilities of his day job.

"Then, one day, I was supposed to go to this weeklong meeting, and I just couldn't do it. I quit," says Patrick. "When I told my boss what I wanted to do, he laughed and said that I would never make it."

But Patrick's boss was wrong. Patrick's income as a motivational speaker has now surpassed what he was making in the corporate world, and his book, *Creating Your Own Destiny* (www.createyourowndestiny .com), has sold hundreds of thousands of copies. How was he able to do it? "I attribute my drive to what I learned growing up in the world of competitive athletics," Patrick says. "I always pushed myself to achieve whatever I set my mind to, and I never gave up no matter what. It's not over until I win or I die."

Today, Patrick speaks weekly at events and conferences large and small, and he's his own boss. "I'm able to coach my boys' sports teams, and we take a family trip to Hawaii every year that's paid for by my business," he says. "I dream of someday living on a sixty-foot yacht in the South Pacific and doing my speeches via satellite or the occasional airport." Patrick coaches his audiences to see all jobs as temporary, not to take failure in the business world personally, and to rally in the face of hard circumstances. "Taking your career into your own hands and doing something independently isn't easy," he says. You won't maintain your perfect credit rating, and it will take you three times longer than you anticipate and cost three times more. But the ability to control your own livelihood is priceless."

Norene
From Customer Service Representative to Professional Musician

Norene's career in customer service began while she was still a student in business administration at California State University. Working for a small publishing company, she took phone orders and did light computer work. Norene was good at her job, and over the next several years she took on roles with greater responsibility. "Though working in business was never what I really wanted, I did develop valuable skills and experience," she says. "For example, I learned how to deal with difficult people without losing my cool and how to manage meeting daily deadlines."

But as time went on, Norene's customer service career became more demanding, and she began to resent it. She was stressed out and depressed, and misfortune in her personal life was about to take center stage. When Norene was thirty-six, her mother was diagnosed with lung cancer and lived just four months. Then, sixteen months later, her father also passed away. Just when Norene thought her grief would overwhelm her, she was further devastated by the news that she had breast cancer.

Norene instantly went into survival mode and gathered information so that she could be educated when she met with her doctors. Norene was lucky that her tumor was caught at an early stage—she had a lumpectomy and then daily radiation treatment for eight weeks. The treatment was inconvenient and exhausting, but Norene took one day at a time and tried her best to keep going. When she recovered enough to take just one pill twice a day, Norene knew that she didn't want to live another day doing work that left her unfulfilled.

Norene had always loved to sing and play the piano. At the beginning of her career, music was still a major part of her life. "I'd sing five nights a week at local restaurants, work as an organist and choir accompanist for a church, and provide music for weddings," she says. But gradually, Norene decreased the time she devoted to it in order to focus on her day job. She'd dreamed of making music a full-time career and performing as a professional singer-songwriter, but didn't consider this a realistic proposition until faced with her parents'—and her own—mortality.

Using her savings, Norene quit her customer service job and applied for work as an accompanist and vocal coach in the local school districts. She also started teaching for a performing arts studio. "I knew I wanted to work for myself, so I told everyone I knew that I was available to teach piano and voice from my home," says Norene. Over the next few years, Norene held several school-based positions and taught dozens of students privately. "It was busy and tiring, and also financially challenging because I often didn't have a steady paycheck, but I loved it and knew I wanted to grow my business. I was willing to do whatever it took, and frankly, it didn't feel like work to me."

Meanwhile, Norene had been writing her own songs on the side, and a friend allowed her to use her recording studio to produce two CDs of original music. "It was the most exciting and fulfilling thing I've ever done and I learned so much about myself and grew so much as a musician as a result of that experience," she says. She frequently traveled from her home in Fresno, California, to Los Angeles to attend music conferences and classes, and Norene knew that if she was really going to give her new career a fair shot, she was going to have to relocate. "I was scared," she admits. "I had to sell my house and leave my hometown and friends behind. And in L.A., I was forced to rebuild my teaching business from the ground up."

Norene faced this challenge with the same determination she had used to overcome her illness and grief. She looked back on her customer service career and employed many of the things she'd learned about how a good business operates and grows. She joined a local Chamber of Commerce and went to every networking event she heard about, and in a short period of time, she progressed from the unemployment line to teaching choir at an elementary school, seeing eighteen students privately, playing keyboard and singing with a church praise band, and performing her original music regularly in the greater L.A. area as Tyler Noren. Norene claims that her soft rock/pop/contemporary sound is influenced by Alanis Morissette, Aerosmith, Barbra Streisand, Sheryl Crow, and Bon Jovi, and her goal for this year is to open her own music studio and to produce and perform a new CD.

As her new career blossoms, Norene often reflects on the journey that brought her here. "Before my cancer, I felt like life was something to be endured. Now I know that we are so much stronger and braver than we realize, and we are capable of achieving such happiness if we just trust our hearts and follow the paths that bring us joy," she says. "When you have a genuine passion that you want to share with the world, people will be supportive. I have received so much help from new and old friends who have been there for me and given me extra strength and encouraging words during this tough transition."

Norene credits those years of darkness with giving her the courage to change her life. After surviving breast cancer and the deaths of her parents, she knew that her unhappiness with her job was something she could control, and that if she worked hard and maintained a positive attitude, she could have the career outcome she wanted. "I'd tell others that the most important thing is to believe in yourself, and to remember that you have something of value to offer," she says. "Once you start to experience life that way, you'll never want to do it differently."

Jason
From Corporate IT Manager to Career Product Developer

As a college student in Idaho, thirty-three-year-old Jason always had a hankering for business, but at the time, many young professionals who wanted to make money were pursuing careers in computers. Jason was no exception. After a short stint as a clerk at the FBI, Jason got his degree in computer science and took a job as a Web programmer at Simplot, a privately held food and agribusiness corporation in Boise, Idaho.

Because Jason was good at what he did, he quickly received an even better opportunity as an IT manager at Varsity Contractors, a Boise-based facility services management firm offering janitorial, landscaping maintenance, construction, lighting, plumbing, and electrical work. It was the year 2000, and Jason made his mark by converting all of Varsity's employees—who were making do with just a few dial-up, America Online accounts—to high-speed Internet access.

All the while, Jason had gotten his MBA, had married, and was raising a family. Using his newfound business knowledge, he helped Varsity to negotiate the acquisition of an accounting software firm. In the deal, Jason earned the title of chief information officer of the new company. "Unfortunately, though the company had been around in some shape or form for a number of years, we had some of the problems more typical of a start-up—like an immature product, a small staff, and little funding," says Jason. Nevertheless, Jason did what he could to make the new company a success, including increasing one division's revenue by 500 percent. The organization rewarded him by naming him general manager.

Jason was on top of the world. He was the youngest person he knew to be making money in the six figures, and during his few short years in the IT world he had compiled a résumé that was quite impressive. But his good fortune was short-lived. When Jason was ordered to cut operating costs and didn't, he was let go. "I thought these people were my friends," he says. "It was ugly, and I was bitter. But I'm not a person who gets depressed, and I loved my work. I thought that with my credentials, surely I'd have something even better before my six-week severance package ran out." Quickly, though, Jason saw that finding a job commensurate with his experience wasn't nearly as easy as he thought it would be. "I went from being this person with clout to being a nobody who couldn't even get a junior HR person to return my calls," Jason says. "My job search was a mess, and even as the months passed it seemed like there were no viable opportunities in sight."

Jason's personal life began to take a beating. "My wife and I didn't talk to each other anymore. My kids would pray at the dinner table that Daddy would get to work safely because I couldn't bear to tell them that their loser of a dad hadn't gone to a job in months," says Jason. And the money was running out. "We had unemployment, but it wasn't enough. We had three kids and another baby on the way, and we had to rely on food vouchers from our church and assistance from our families to scrape by." Then, one day, Jason had enough. "I decided that even though there were lots of things I liked about corporate life and IT, never again could I allow a single company to dictate whether or not I could provide for my family. That was when I drafted my first business plan."

The plan was for an entrepreneurial venture called JibberJobber (www.jibberjobber.com), a Web-based contact management system that provides a job-hunting tool set to keep track of and manage résumés, cover letters, interviews, recruiters, leads, contacts, action items, and follow-ups. "All of my previous experience in Web design and development, marketing, sales, management, and customer support contributed to the launch of the new business," says Jason. "And when I went out and pitched the product to government agencies, associations, career coaches, and colleges, the feedback I received was really encouraging."

As Jason signs up licensing partners by the dozen and increases his profile as a thought leader in the online career advice sphere, he has never been happier. "Career change is something that was forced on me, but looking back now, I feel that it was meant to be. Because I wasn't getting a job despite being overqualified, it seems that there was a higher power telling me that this is what I was supposed to do," he says. "Since I started the business, I haven't used an alarm clock. I want to wake up in the morning and get out there. It's so invigorating being part of a small business community that has a 'just do it' mentality. There's none of the bureaucracy of the corporate world, and that's refreshing."

Jason encourages other young professionals to look at their setbacks as opportunities. "One thing I've learned is that you have to have an open mind," says Jason. "No matter how hard you try, your career won't happen exactly the way you plan. No kid thinks he'll put in time working, for instance, in a funeral parlor. All you can do is pay attention to the signs along the way, and you'll see that your destiny is out there."

Nicole
From Management Consultant to Adoption Counselor

When it came to her schooling, thirty-nine-year-old Nicole always did the safe thing. Her education was as well-rounded as well-rounded gets—she earned her undergraduate degree from Lehigh University in Bethlehem, Pennsylvania, with a major in computer science and minors in religion and urban studies. Nicole's first job out of school was with Andersen Consulting (now Accenture). "I got it the traditional way—by interviewing on campus through the career services office," she says. "It was a very prestigious job, the kind my parents had always expected me to get. I knew I'd made them proud."

As a systems developer with Andersen, Nicole realized she preferred strategy work to programming, so she decided to go back to school for her MBA. "The bureaucracy of the corporate world was making me miserable, but for some reason I still focused on working for large organizations," she admits. While pursuing her advanced degree at Cornell University in Ithaca, New York, Nicole did an internship with McNeil Pharmaceutical (now Ortho-McNeil-Janssen Pharmaceutical), and after graduation, took a brand management position with Warner-Lambert (now part of Pfizer.) At Warner, she learned about the various components of marketing and how to manage teams of people who were older and more experienced. Nicole was just beginning to think that she could be satisfied working at a large company when her husband's career took them to Atlanta.

In the south, Nicole started working for Eastman Kodak, and once again she found herself disillusioned. The organization didn't put much emphasis on training managers, and despite her efforts to seek out interesting projects, Nicole repeatedly encountered difficult bosses. She knew in her heart that the corporate world was not for her and that she needed to find a career that would reward her abilities and allow her to choose her colleagues, but it was easier said than done. After all the hard work and education Nicole had undertaken to get to this point, she simply didn't have the nerve to walk away.

Meanwhile, Nicole and her husband had started trying to have a baby, and they were gradually realizing that it was going to be harder than they thought. Nicole was a carrier of a genetic syndrome, fragile X, which left her practically no chance of getting pregnant on her own. She tried a cycle of in vitro fertilization, but because fragile X carriers typically respond poorly, the procedure was unsuccessful. Devastated, Nicole and her husband decided to pursue egg donorship. "Our donor produced so many eggs that we called her the Easter Bunny, but my uterine lining wasn't good and that cycle failed, too," Nicole says. "Fortunately, we had frozen embryos left and the next two cycles worked, resulting in my daughter and son. They were born nineteen months apart, but are technically twins since they were conceived on the same day."

This period was the most stressful one in Nicole's life. "I wouldn't trade my children for the world, but I can't imagine going through those treatments again—the pain, the inconvenience, the medications, and the side effects," she says. "Women going through infertility have the same levels of depression as those battling terminal illness. It called into question my whole reason for being on earth and impacted all of my personal and professional relationships, because people who haven't been through it can't understand why you don't want to attend a baby shower or why you have a doctor's appointment every morning for three months straight."

At the end of her four-year battle with infertility, Nicole knew it was time for a major change. "I couldn't go back and pretend to care about marketing cameras when I knew there were so many more important issues in life," she says. "I also knew that the unhappy woman I was working in the corporate world was not the person I wanted my children to be raised by." Nicole and her husband had come close to adopting, and she found that she had a talent for navigating the system. She began volunteering with adoption professionals, and using the contacts she made and her insider knowledge, was able to guide friends quickly and successfully through the often overwhelming and confusing adoption process.

Nicole and her family decided to relocate to Florida, and Nicole used the move as a jumping-off point to turn her passion into a full-time venture. She established the Adoption Consultancy (www .theadoptionconsultancy.com), a business in which she provides prospective parents with support and guidance, information about procedures, risk assessment, and a customized plan for moving forward. Now Nicole spends her days networking with adoption agencies and attorneys, and educating parents—allaying their fears and helping them to make decisions that are right for them. "My first consultation with a client often lasts about four hours," Nicole says. "Usually it's by phone, but for local clients, it's in person. These meetings are rewarding and satisfying because I immediately see my positive impact in the relief that clients feel and the sense of peace they develop."

Thanks to the time she spent as an adoption apprentice, the constant support of her husband, and her innate attention to detail, Nicole's transition to her new career was relatively seamless. "We saved as much money as we could before I left my corporate job so that the business didn't need to make money for the first year or so. I also continued doing freelance work on the side to keep afloat." She claims that her biggest obstacles were fear and self-doubt. "I was also worried about minor logistical issues such as how I was going to accept credit cards, but working on those details each day gave me confidence for the bigger tasks."

Nicole feels that the most important factor in her successful career change was the inner desire that resulted from her battle with infertility. This desire drove her to overcome challenges that might have stopped her in the past. "I had a marketing background so marketing my business was not a problem, but I wasn't as comfortable with the sales side of things. I simply had to push myself because the alternative of going back to the corporate world was now unacceptable to me," she says. Nicole encourages others who have faced adversity to harness it to chart new paths. "When deciding how to proceed from a career setback, identify what's most meaningful to you. If you don't know what it is, open yourself up to possibilities through volunteer work and new experiences. Once you've hit on it, pursue it wholeheartedly and success will follow."

David
From Architectural Engineer to Teacher

Born in a rough neighborhood in the Bronx, New York, and educated in New York City's public school system, David was, perhaps not surprisingly, exposed to the wrong type of crowd. "A lot of my peers got caught up in drugs and went to prison," David says. "Lucky for me, my parents were a major influence. They encouraged me to keep up with sports and church, and when they saw me going down the wrong path, they sent me to boarding school in North Carolina." This school, which might be the last African American institution of its kind in the country, paved the way for David to attend North Carolina A&T University. Following in his father's footsteps, David studied architectural engineering. "There's no doubt that I was ill prepared for university, but somehow I got through."

Upon graduation, David returned to his home base in New York and took a job with the firm Gibbs & Cox. The company focused on naval and marine architecture, so David obtained a government security clearance and spent his days designing ships, frigates, and destroyers. His next position with the New York City Board of Education allowed him to pursue his love of building creation. His team was responsible for rebuilding old schools and designing new ones, and the assignment presented a crash course in construction and other critical skills. "Architecture prepares you for a lot of different careers because you're a constant observer of how people live and act," David tells us. "You have to manage people and projects, and also understand the legal side of things. And of course, architects have to be organized and able to multitask. I was multitasking way before it was cool."

David married his college sweetheart and moved to Detroit to be near her family. Once again he was able to score an architectural gig that benefited the public good. "At BEI Associates, I surveyed day-care centers to make sure they were up to par," David says. "I wrote reports about my findings and ran various construction projects. It was a good job and I was happy." But, as David learned, all good things come to an end. He was twenty-eight years old and supporting a one-year-old and a wife who wasn't working when the economy took a downturn and David's major client stopped working on his project. He was laid off. "I couldn't believe it. I'd been so secure in my career, and now I was worried about how I'd keep the house going."

Still reeling, David hustled to start a CAD (computer-aided design) and drafting services business. In between his jobs completing projects for local architects, David took a part-time position as a CAD teacher's assistant at the Breithaupt Career and Technical Center to earn a little extra money. To his surprise, David discovered he liked teaching high school students and giving back to the community in a different way, but at first he wasn't motivated to go back to school to obtain his certification. Gradually, though, distress over the family's finances kicked in. "My clients' checks started bouncing, and my wife told me to get a real job," David says. "We'd both realized that I wasn't savvy enough to maintain my own business and worry about things like cash flow."

After receiving a master's degree in teaching from Wayne State University in Detroit, David became a CAD program manager at the Randolph Career and Technical Center. He spent the next several years building up the program, establishing a robotics team and helping students to enter a host of national architecture competitions. "I received a grant from Ford to start a Saturday High initiative, in which I taught industrial design to high schoolers who were interested in becoming automotive engineers," he says proudly. "It was very rewarding to keep in touch with students and witness their successes."

David's gifts soon earned him the teaching world's highest credential—National Board Certification. Shortly afterward, he won the Milken Educator of the Year Award and was promoted to supervisor of career and technical education for Detroit Public Schools. "Now I get to oversee all sorts of programs, from auto body and printing to electronics and even aviation! I get to go out to the schools and talk with the students, which I love," David says. "It's not always easy, though. I obviously don't know about all of these disciplines, and getting money from the government and ensuring compliance with regulations is challenging."

David is sympathetic to those experiencing career setbacks. "Human beings don't like change, but because of the world we live in, things get shaken up," he says. "We will all have a bunch of different careers in our lifetimes, and some of those careers don't even exist yet. The best you can do is create a foundation of business skills, and, if you're in the midst of a job loss, find something pertaining to those skills that you can be the expert at." David is quick to admit that individuals respond differently to hardship. "But no matter who you are, you'll be better off if you seek the support of your family and immerse yourself in something you love, something where you could put in hours and hours without it feeling cumbersome."

Unless fate has other plans, David will stay in the education world for the foreseeable future. In addition to his other talents, he has recently discovered a knack for writing. "I'm working on a piece about how project-based education can help students who don't do as well on standardized tests," he says. "Wish me luck!"

☞ Self-Reflection: Is a Setback Your Motivation?

- Has a personal crisis caused you to reevaluate what's really important?

- Have recent events in your life left you wondering why you chose your job in the first place?
- After being fired or laid off, are you now finding that you have less of a desire to get another job in your field?
- Has misfortune given you more courage to pursue a path you previously thought was impossible?
- Do you feel like you've recently had a string of bad luck?
- Are feelings of depression and anxiety currently coloring your view of the world?
- Have frequent feelings of hopelessness drained your motivation at work?
- Have your family and friends been telling you that you're stuck in a rut?
- Are you afraid to make a career change because things are already bad enough and you're worried about making things worse?
- Do you ever wish you didn't have to have a job at all and that you could just stay home?

👍 If you answered "Yes" to two or more of these questions, you may be experiencing a setback that is affecting your work. Read on for advice and tools you can use to get through this tough period and come out more satisfied with your career than you were before!

☞ Putting the Change to Work

Accept what has happened: When you wake up in the morning, your first inclination may be to deny the situation. This is completely normal. In her 1969 book *On Death and Dying*, Elisabeth Kübler-Ross popularized the five discrete stages in which people cope with grief and tragedy—and you guessed it, denial was number one. However, people overcome grief by moving on from this attitude, eventually reaching the last and most healthy stage of acceptance. "The sooner you can be in the same place as the setback, and not feel like you need to *do* anything—explain it away, fix it, judge it, or compensate for it—the sooner you will be able to use the experience to your advantage," says Michael Weitz of Ovation Coaching.

Reconfigure your perspective: Failure is not the mythical monster it's cracked up to be. In his book *The Power of Failure*, author Charles Manz says that while sometimes failure is tied to a lack of competence to perform in the face of a specific challenge, it is often the means for life's greatest breakthroughs and successes. "Optimistic thinking has sometimes gotten a bad rap, but research has found that we can live happier, healthier, and more successful lives if we can learn to discover the opportunities in problems," advises Manz. He also advocates redefining what constitutes failure and what constitutes success. Viewing failure, for instance, as a falling short because of ineptness, deficiency, or negligence, and as a bad thing that should be avoided, mourned, or punished, is not particularly helpful. Instead, why not look at it as a short-term, unexpected result that provides an opening for creative change and innovation? Similarly, success should not be looked upon as a revered shrine of achievement, indicating superior ability that requires no further learning, or performance that is devoid of flaws or weakness. Rather, success is an outcome of short-term failures and involves an ongoing sequence of life-improving results.

Take time to heal: Before you rush into a new job or a new career, allow yourself to feel the common emotions of disappointment, rejection, worry, and bitterness. "Feelings of uncertainty can linger," says Bradley Richardson, the author of *Career Comeback: 8 Steps to Getting Back on Your Feet When You're Fired, Laid Off, or Your Business Venture Has Failed*, in an article for the *Wall Street Journal*. "It's like a relationship ending. If you were badly burned, you'll likely remain guarded until a new situation re-establishes your trust." Recognize, though, that you won't always feel this badly. The only thing that's certain about human emotions is that they change constantly, and even when you've experienced hardship, your mood is likely to pick up on its own with a little time.

Consider whether your career is really the problem: People who suffer from clinical depression or anxiety often have a negative view of their careers regardless of the circumstances. For instance, you might feel like a delinquent at your job even in the face of a glowing performance review. Before you act too hastily, assess whether your current unhappiness extends to all areas of your life—for example, your relationships with family and friends, your hobbies, and your religion. If so, you might be better served by the counsel of a trained therapist. Search for qualified professionals at the Association for Behavioral and Cognitive Therapies (www.abct.org) or the Academy of Cognitive Therapy (www.academyofct.org) websites.

Recognize the facts: When a setback darkens your doorstep, the tendency is to feel like your bad luck will last forever. But, as we mentioned above, the key to viewing setbacks and failures in a healthy light is to think short-term. By keeping in mind that the situation is temporary, you'll be strong enough to take the necessary steps to overcome the misfortune. In the meantime, try to analyze the scenario from an objective point of view. A setback may signal that this isn't the right path for you to be on, and may indicate that it's time for a drastic change. For instance, if you've been trying to make it as an actor for ten years and still haven't gotten a part despite auditioning for dozens of roles, perhaps it's time to rethink whether acting is the ideal career for you. On the other hand, a career obstacle may mean that you simply need to dust yourself off and try again. Just because you were laid off from your job doesn't mean you have no talent for the work. The layoff could easily be the result of business realities completely out of your control and might have nothing to do with you personally. No matter what the facts say, though, look for ways to take personal accountability for your situation. See what you can learn: Perhaps there were actions you took or behaviors you exhibited that you can avoid in your next endeavor. For example, if you were fired because you didn't follow through on work-related tasks, that lack of commitment is likely to follow you from job to job, or career to career. Don't let it.

Reach out to your support network: During a crisis, it always helps to know you are not alone and that you are justified in feeling the way you do. Instead of withdrawing from the people you care about, make an effort to connect with them, lean on them for support, and count on them for a good laugh or some much-needed time off the couch. The people who know you best can help you take a step back from an emotionally charged situation and view it in a more constructive light. Your network of friends and family is most critical, but you can receive comfort and insight from spiritual support systems and prayer as well. In fact, just being around other people can brighten your mood, so even if you're having a really tough time, book at least one engagement a week that involves going out in public. It may seem like a chore to get in the car and go, but once you're there, you'll be surprised at how much better you feel.

Consider what you'll do next: Maybe now is the time to assess if the work you've been involved in truly motivates you, or if there is something out there that would be a better fit. "Ask yourself if you are the type of professional or executive you want to be. Are you the kind of worker your ideal employer would seek out? If not, consider what's missing and what steps you need to take to fit that profile," says Richardson. "You're now a clean slate and have an opportunity to reinvent yourself and start fresh." If you need help with this process, seek out a respected career coach or spend some time with the self-reflection exercises in this book and those recommended in the resource toolkit.

Conquer fear and self-doubt: Even if we theoretically understand the best way to proceed and think we've healed sufficiently, the aftereffects of a setback can still be paralyzing. Don't allow the little voice in your head that questions your talents and abilities to take over, and deliberately put yourself in situations that will prompt to you to face your fears and insecurities head-on. "Go beyond your comfort zone," says Lybi Ma, in an article for *Psychology Today*. "Go after that job you think you can't do, because doing so will build self-esteem and resilience." I've followed Ma's advice myself, and I'll give you an example. Since I became an author, I have spoken in public at least a hundred times, and even though I have been told that I am a competent speaker, things don't go universally well at my events. Once, while I was pregnant, I felt very sick during a speech, and another time, when I forgot my notes and had to improvise, I came across as less articulate and more flustered than usual. These situations led me to experience some anxiety around public speaking last year, and I was tempted to avoid booking engagements. I realized, though, that I wouldn't be taking advantage of the invaluable opportunity to personally share my messages with large groups of readers if I didn't get back out there. Even though I was scared, I stretched my wings with different and even more challenging events, and eventually, after I was able to proceed successfully, my fear subsided.

Embrace risk: People who have experienced setbacks often tend to avoid future failure at all costs. But here's the thing. A willingness to accept risk and the possibility of additional challenges is the quickest way to discover the most fruitful outcome. I have done some work with Microsoft, and Bill Gates is widely considered to be the most successful businessman on earth. But he would not have gotten where he is today without trying various tactics to see what would work and what wouldn't. In his speeches and articles, he has told of the significant investment in time and dollars that went into failed projects like the Omega database and a joint operating system with IBM. But if it weren't for Omega, we wouldn't have Microsoft Access, and if it weren't for the discontinued IBM effort, Windows would not have progressed to its current superproduct status.

Hire a life coach: Life coaching is an interactive process that helps individuals achieve better results in their personal and professional lives. Coaches work with clients in all areas, including business, career, finances, health, and relationships. They are certified and trained to listen, to observe, and to customize their approach to your individual needs. The life coaching process typically begins with a short interview over the phone or in person so that the coach can assess your current challenges, priorities, and desired results. Subsequent sessions may last about sixty minutes, during which your coach will help you set better goals, take more action, make better decisions, and more fully use your natural strengths. In between scheduled meeting times, your coach may ask you to complete specific exercises or read materials that support behavior change and goal achievement. Check out websites such as www.lifecoach.com and www.coachfederation.org to learn more about life coaching.

Commit yourself to a new endeavor: Preparing for a new career—or a new job in which you're afforded a fresh perspective—can provide you with a sorely needed dose of enthusiasm. Even if you're tempted to sit around the house all day, recognize that laziness will actually make you feel worse. Work hard at your transition, treating your networking and research activities as part of a full-time job, and break down the huge project of "changing your career" into smaller tasks so it doesn't seem so overwhelming. You'll also want to get to know individuals who are going through a similar experience and are handling their plight in a healthy, action-based way. Follow their lead in creating timelines and to-do lists, meeting contacts for lunch, going to support group meetings, and reconfiguring your résumé and marketing materials so that they showcase your recent learnings. Then...

Be patient: It is human nature to want to skip the learning stages associated with long-term career fulfillment, and the more hardship you've experienced, the more eager you are to turn things around sooner rather than later. Charles Manz tells the story of his efforts to learn tai chi. In anticipation of the health benefits he would receive, Manz was eager to master his technique right away. Despite his instructor's advice that he take it slow and start by learning one or two poses at a time, he tried to master a whole form in a month instead of the year it typically requires. Because he hadn't been patient with the process, Manz was eventually forced to work doubly hard to relearn his poses in a technically correct manner. I'll admit that I'm guilty of the same thing, but I've realized over time that every time I rush into something in an effort to get away from negative feelings, my short-cuts cost me dearly and the healing process takes even longer.

Showcase what you've overcome: When interviewing or talking to contacts about your career change, don't hide the fact that you've experienced a setback. Instead, package it in a way that allows people to see how resilient you are. You'd be surprised, but usually job candidates who express an ability to learn from their mistakes are considered more desirable than those who act as if they're perfect. While writing this book, two different sources told me about how NASA used prior failure as a measure for selecting new recruits for the *Apollo 11* lunar mission. NASA deliberately sought out those who had bounced back from at least one major setback because it wanted astronauts who, over the course of their lives, had developed enough inner strength and resources to withstand the stress and challenges associated with flying to the moon. Given that, I wonder how many of those astronauts still regret their past failures.

☞ Exercise: Overcoming Your Setback

• In your own words, describe the negative event(s) that has (have) occurred in your life in the last twelve months.

• How has that event made you feel (angry, betrayed, frustrated, etc.) and why?

• How has this event impacted how you view your career?

• List three steps you can take today to heal from this event.

• Name two people you can reach out to for support, and a deadline for getting in touch with them.

• List three hobbies, causes, or careers that you find interesting or feel enthusiastic about.

- Brainstorm three steps you might take to parlay one of these into a new job or career.

☞ Resource Toolkit

Websites

Academy of Cognitive Therapy: www.academyofct.org
Association for Behavioral and Cognitive Therapies: www.abct.org
Beliefnet: www.beliefnet.com
DailyStrength: dailystrength.org
International Coach Federation: www.coachfederation.org
Mayo Clinic Stress Management: www.mayoclinic.com/
    health/stress-management/MY00435
PsychCentral: psychcentral.com
U.S. Department of Labor (unemployment): www.dol.gov

Books

The Relaxation & Stress Reduction Workbook (Martha Davis, Elizabeth
    Robbins Eshelman, and Matthew McKay)
Self-Coaching: The Powerful Program to Beat Anxiety and Depression
    (Joseph Luciani)
The Power of Failure: 27 Ways to Turn Life's Setbacks into Success
    (Charles Manz)
We Got Fired! (Harvey MacKay)
*Career Comeback: 8 Steps to Getting Back on Your Feet When You're Fired,
    Laid Off, or Your Business Venture Has Failed* (Bradley Richardson)
The Power of Now: A Guide to Spiritual Enlightenment (Eckhart Tolle)
*The Power of Adversity: Tough Times Can Make You Stronger, Wiser, and
    Better* (Al Weatherhead and Fred Feldman)

Talent

If you have a talent, use it in every which way possible.
Don't hoard it. Don't dole it out like a miser.
Spend it lavishly like a millionaire intent on going broke.

—Brendan Francis, writer

Talent comes in many forms, so as I was preparing to write this chapter, I asked a bunch of people who they thought of as "talented." By and large, they listed artists. This makes sense when you think about the contestants that comprise the hit reality show *America's Got Talent*. The majority are singers and musicians.

You may be working at a job you don't enjoy while sitting on an explosive talent because you believe your odds of becoming a successful artist are too slim and that nobody *actually* makes money. And before now, I might have been tempted to agree with you. However, the National Endowment for the Arts just released a nationwide study on artists' demographic and employment patterns in the twenty-first century. Numbering almost two million, working artists are one of the largest classes in the nation, only slightly smaller than the U.S. military's active-duty and reserve personnel.

Blogger Aaron Stanton of BookLamp.org proposes that it's not as difficult as one thinks to make it to the top of the most desirable artistic professions. "Let's say, for example, that you want to become a famous actor," writes Stanton. "We'll define famous as having one of the top 200 acting jobs in Hollywood. You might think that millions of people want to become famous actors, but the truth is, as soon as you make the decision to pursue the career full time, you're only competing against those who are doing the same."

Stanton uses the NEA data on working artists to illustrate that if you're a talented actor, a good networker, and decent-looking, your chances of becoming accomplished in Hollywood are better than you might expect. "If you have the right characteristics and you stand up now, walk out of your door, and go become an actor, your odds of landing a spot in that Top 200 are 1 in 23, because so few people really do it," he explains. "But if you just nod, think what I say is interesting, and then go make yourself lunch—then welcome to the millions. Your odds are entirely determined by your next moves."

This chapter showcases individuals with talents they just couldn't suppress, who had the gumption to go out into the world and snag the coveted careers they deserved. The artist stories you'll read echo some of the trends uncovered by NEA's study, including that artists are entrepreneurial and much more likely to be self-employed, that opportunities for artistic employment are greater in metropolitan areas, and that one-fifth of all artists in the United States live in Los Angeles, New York, Chicago, Boston, and Washington, D.C.

In addition to artists, athletes and chefs were frequently mentioned in my informal survey of talented individuals, so I've included the stories of a media planner turned martial arts professional and a painter turned chef, and in the "Putting the Change to Work" section, you'll find advice for breaking into a number of creative fields, including the rarefied ones of athletics and food. Enjoy the journey, and remember that every time you take a step forward, you're increasing the likelihood that your talent will soon be witnessed by the multitudes!

Adam
From Investment Banker to Children's Songwriter

Since junior high, Adam was on a path to a finance career. His uncle was very successful in the field, and pressure was placed on Adam by his family. A career in the arts was never entertained, so to speak. Adam attended Miami University in Oxford, Ohio, and received a bachelor of science degree in finance and economics. He followed that with a master's degree in business administration from New York University's prestigious Stern School of Business and soon became a chartered financial analyst. Not surprisingly, Adam's first job out of school involved working for his uncle, who ran a commodities trading fund. "After spending some time as a trading assistant, I went on to work for various investment banks trading currencies," says Adam. "I gradually climbed the ladder and after a few years, was the senior trader at Banque Paribas who had created the yen trading desk."

Adam's career eventually led him in the direction of equity research and management, working with hedge funds and asset managers. Though he felt he was learning a great deal in the financial industry, he couldn't ignore the pull to do something more creative. Adam is naturally extroverted and growing up had been the star of all the school plays, had sung in the choir, and had even won a state debate championship. So it wasn't a surprise when he began entertaining his trading desk colleague with character voices.

In the back of his mind, Adam knew he had an innate talent for creative expression, and was perhaps better suited for it than finance. But in his twenties, there was no question that he would stick with the career he'd been groomed for all his life. "Finance was always secure, a sure way to provide for myself. I was willing to take risks when dealing with the markets, but not when it came to my own life," Adam relates. "Considering a path outside of finance was completely foreign and impossible to me for a long time."

Then Adam married composer and pianist Belinda, who had a Ph.D. in music composition. As they anticipated the birth of their first child, Adam and Belinda shopped for classical music DVDs suitable for babies. "Allowing for the possibility that our genes might not do it all, we gravitated toward products that could turn a creature that likes to chew on a burp cloth into a genius like Einstein or Mozart. To say we were disappointed with the synthesized classical music out there was an understatement," they say on their website. Adam and Belinda felt that as a team, they could do better. The duo created Juno Baby (www.junobaby.com), an educational DVD, apparel, and toy company for children ages five and under—named for their daughter, Juno.

Although it was tempting to simply let their creative juices flow,

Adam and Belinda did their homework. Unlike competitors who use electronic sounds to mimic classical music, Juno Baby's music is live and performed by orchestral musicians. The content, which involves speaking directly to children through characters, soliciting active participation, and providing ample opportunities to respond, was based on a language production and vocabulary study published in *American Behavioral Scientist*. The Juno Baby cast of puppets is performed by alumni of *Fraggle Rock* and includes quirky and memorable characters that young children can understand and relate to.

Adam has his hands in all aspects of the business. "I do character voiceovers, writing, directing, production, and composition, and all the while run a start-up company, which involves everything from PR and graphic design to accounting and IT," he says. "I love what I do, and my passion for music is what allowed it to develop into more than just a hobby."

Adam credits his equally talented wife with being the catalyst for change in their lives. He could have made a transition earlier, but admittedly, he got in his own way. "I thought that the world was narrow, and that I wasn't talented enough," he says. "I identified myself only with the finance world, and equated it with status and success. In my opinion, any other path was a lesser path."

Now in his thirties raising a preschool-age Juno in Northern California, Adam couldn't be prouder of what he has created. Not only has Juno Baby won an Emmy Award for original music and received coverage in nearly every parenting magazine across the globe, but it has also been financially solvent enough to donate products and profits to charitable organizations such as the Ronald McDonald House and St. Jude Children's Research Hospital, and to create an online community for parents to discuss the benefits of music education and entertainment for young children.

Adam tells us that major career change in pursuit of a talent absolutely requires the support of a spouse and family. "You must also have courage, confidence, and the faith that doing what you love will support you," he says. "As long as you have the skill, it will happen."

Allison
From Marketer to Comedienne

At thirty-four, Allison has experienced a lot in her life, including twelve years of Catholic school, three attempts at an anthropology degree, and a stint in beauty school—all while in her early twenties. When she finally finished college, Allison took a job at an alternative health clinic. "I had been sick, so I worked out a deal with the doctor to pay off my bill by teaching nutrition to Amish patients," Allison says. "It was a blessing because I learned so much, and in return, was empowered to teach others."

Allison then ventured into the corporate world with a position at an international marketing firm. "I hated the job, but it did push me to take my life more seriously," she says. "I also improved my computer skills, and my 'keep moving even if they hang up on you' sales skills. I became a better listener, and I learned that just because someone is dressed in Kenneth Cole doesn't mean she knows what the hell she's doing."

Allison's marketing career taught her to look beyond appearances and see the professionalism, creativity, and productivity of her co-workers. Unfortunately, she also realized that her overall unhappiness with her job was resulting in depression, weight gain, and overspending. Her dissatisfaction led her to attend workshops, read books on different religions, and see a counselor. "A major change happened when I was asked by my counselor: 'If I could do anything, what would it be?' and I said 'stand-up comedy.'" When the counselor didn't scoff at the idea, Allison started thinking. She mustered the courage to talk to working comics and club bartenders about what she wanted. "I truly believe that most people want to help and see others succeed," Allison says. Two weeks later, she was onstage.

Stationed in Columbus, Ohio, at the time, Allison entered the city's Funniest Person finals, and to her surprise placed second. She followed that with other contest wins, and it was this validation of her talent that led her to believe she could actually make a living in comedy. "It seemed easy because I had so many beginner's green lights telling me I was on the right path," she says. "But I was also naïve. I thought there were Hollywood agents at every open-mic event waiting to pick out and groom new talent!"

As she gained more experience, Allison realized that actual stage time is only a small part of being a working comedienne. "There's also writing, networking, finding and creating shows, and marketing yourself," she says. "The day-to-day job involves all of these things, plus taking workshops and contacting bookers." Allison decided to train at the highly regarded Second City. She moved to Chicago on September 10, 2001, and the next day, nothing seemed funny.

Nevertheless, in the years since, Allison has established a thriving career. She describes herself as equal parts of every *Facts of Life* character, including Mrs. Garrett. She recently wrote, directed, and performed a one-woman show called *Hello, My Name Is... You* and has worked in comedy clubs in New York, Columbus, Detroit, and Louisville. In 2005, Allison co-founded the popular comedy troupe the Chicago Underground, which allows up-and-comers to showcase their talent in a professional atmosphere.

Allison's story shows that even people who experience success quickly have their doubts. "I do catch myself feeling jealous at times, but have found that it is very destructive and defeating. I have to remind myself that there are enough opportunities and shows out there for all of us," she says. "Another thing I realized is that I don't have to be friends with everyone. I used to stay in conversations that I found offensive or just plain boring so that I could feel like I was part of the comedy community. I was being counterproductive by giving away my time."

Allison claims that she was able to translate her comedic talent into a stream of paying gigs through intuition, persistence, commitment to her spirituality, and knowing when to ask for help. She advises prospective entertainers to do self-reflection and choose mentors carefully before making a transition. "Surround yourself with people who are committed to their goals, and rent movies about world leaders and revolutionaries for inspiration," she says.

She also recommends reading about your industry's history and spending your days being proactive. "Create events that bring you together with the community. I, for example, once emptied my bank account to rent a theater and put on a show based on an idea I had. And don't avoid getting started by taking too many workshops and classes."

"I still feel lost at times," Allison admits. "But I know that the feeling will pass. I pull out some old shows or business cards to get me jump-started again. I'll also explore other mediums like radio, which I enjoy very much." All in all, she is ecstatic about her decision to nourish her talent. "I have grown so much from performing comedy, and I've proven to myself that I can do what I initially thought I was incapable of." One goal for the future? Overcoming her fear of earthquakes. "I want to move to L.A.!" she says.

Jennifer
From Media Planner to Nightclub Owner to Martial Arts Professional

When Jennifer graduated from Fordham University in the Bronx, she only knew that she wanted to work in restaurants. It was, after all, how she'd supported herself in school. "The money was great and it was a very social environment," she says. "But I had the feeling that I should get some type of day job. I wound up being an assistant in a media-buying company." Jennifer mastered core administrative skills but found the job useless otherwise.

Searching for something that was closer to the restaurant world that she loved, Jennifer next went to work for an event space on Rector Street in Manhattan. Her stint in event planning taught her the importance of nailing first impressions and seeking out opportunities to build relationships. Shortly afterward, however, Jennifer's life was overturned by the events of September 11, 2001. "After I almost died on that day, I realized that life is too short. I made some major decisions, including getting involved with a man I normally wouldn't have dated and taking a job as a nightclub manager."

At this time in her life, Jennifer had begun studying martial arts (hapkido). *Hapkido*, translated literally, means "The Way of Harmonizing Life Force Energy," and encompasses physical, emotional, mental, and spiritual development. "Physically, you feel great, but developing

focus, discipline, mental strength, and a sense of peace and empowerment are far greater benefits of the training," Jennifer tells us.

Jennifer was successful at her nightclub job due to her ability to
please clients and make them feel special, but she found that she
couldn't wait to leave work to train in hapkido. "I started to think there
had to be a better way of contributing to society. After all, what was I
doing? Getting twenty-something kids drunk to the point of throwing
up? I wanted to help people get healthy and feel as great as I did after
training in hapkido—strong, confident, aware, and energetic!"

Jennifer's natural talent for martial arts was no surprise to her
father, who is a health nut and martial arts aficionado himself. She
decided to take the first step in making her hobby a career by leaving the nightclub and getting a job at a gym. "My friend got me an
interview at a health club," Jennifer remembers. "I figured I could
teach kickboxing, but he wound up convincing me to become a
personal trainer. I got certified, built up clientele, and a year later
decided that I wanted to build my own practice."

Again, with the spontaneity Jennifer is known for, the twenty-
five-year-old jumped right in. "The lack of income was definitely
an obstacle living in New York City," she says. "I think that this
is probably what holds the majority of people back from switching
careers." And then there was the fear. "What if it doesn't work out?
What if I can't pay my rent? What if at best I just become average? Yuck! However, it turns out that fear is a great motivator. I told
myself that I would do whatever it took to break out of the mold and
refine my skills in a niche market."

As Jennifer created her martial arts practice, Health and the City
(www.healthandthecity.net), one client at a time, she also created the
lifestyle she wanted to live. "I always hated the idea of a nine-to-five
job and preferred to set my own schedule," she says. Now, Jennifer wakes up around 7 A.M. and trains a few clients at their homes.
Returning to her home office, she handles marketing and business
tasks, or runs errands. Her afternoon involves going to the *dojang*
(martial arts studio), where she trains individual clients and teaches
group classes. "The beauty of having my own business is that I can
build programs that I personally derive energy from," she says. "I also

get to travel a lot—training in Montauk, Long Island, in the summer and doing seminars from California and Fiji. It's loads of fun!"

Jennifer says that her confidence has been enhanced by martial arts: "Through self-defense training and meditation and excruciating black belt tests, I knew that I could do anything. Even after I gave my all, there was still more left in me." Jennifer feels that the first step in making a career transition is to envision your current life stretching into the future. "Ask yourself, how would it feel to be in the same career in five or ten years knowing that you have the power to change it now? What you don't want can motivate you as much as what you do want." Her most important piece of advice to those with talent is to ignore the naysayers. "People who are already in your field may try to deflate your dreams so that they can keep you from reaching a higher level than them. Don't listen to them, listen to your intuition."

Jennifer also warns that complacency can be your biggest enemy. "Taking action—any action—is the best way to get unstuck even when you're not sure that the action is the right one. It's a great way to let the universe know that you are ready to move on," she says. Finally, she recommends that talented individuals be flexible and focused, and that they keep up with their education. "Keep monthly and yearly goals hanging in a visible place and review them daily. Get a coach or a mentor and continue to train in your field so you are always at the forefront of the industry."

Today, Jennifer is working on a master's degree and writing a book. And of course, hapkido keeps her as busy as ever. "From my sport, I've learned the concept of flow, and it's a great lesson. When we're not on the right path, it feels like swimming upstream without direction, but when we are doing what we love, we flow through life."

Amy
From Stockbroker to Needlepoint Designer

Cornell University graduate and current thirty-something Amy wasn't any ordinary stockbroker when she graduated from college. She got to work in Italy. "My dad requested that I major in economics so that I'd be employable, but my real passion was languages," she relates. "I studied

Italian for four years, and I wanted to move to Italy at all costs. After networking heavily, I flew overseas and got hired on a short contract."

Amy started as the assistant to the head of a small and scrappy company. Brokers from London and New York City called at all hours with their opinions on markets, stocks, and bonds. Since Amy's boss was rarely in the office, she had to listen and ask questions so she could report back to him. "It was a great way to learn about the industry and about how to value companies," she says. "Since we were so small, I was given a lot more responsibility than I would have had at another firm. We were also very entrepreneurial, which meant that the three of us did everything from research to marketing to buying paper and pens. I saw firsthand what was needed to run a small business."

At the conclusion of her first year, Amy became a stockbroker herself and started to build her own client base. She also became friends with a lot of Italians. When visiting their homes, Amy noticed stunning needlepoint tapestries, and needlepoint-covered chairs and pillows. "These were heirloom pieces that had been in the families for generations and were considered priceless," she explains. "I was fascinated with the intricate patterns and the workmanship that went into each piece."

Amy had trouble adjusting to her new fast-paced schedule as a stockbrocker and became increasingly stressed out. One day, someone mentioned to her that needlepoint was a great stress relief activity. Remembering the beautiful designs she had seen in her friends' homes, she was excited to learn. But while Amy was instantly hooked on this craft that kept her hands busy, calmed her nerves, and put her into a meditation-like state, she also had a hard time finding projects and designs that she wanted to stitch. "I remember very clearly my first visit to a needlepoint store," Amy says. "I spent at least two hours there and couldn't find anything I liked that wasn't outrageously large or expensive. I finally ended up with a kit to stitch an eyeglass case that said 'FORE!' and the O looked like a golf ball."

Amy decided to pursue an MBA at Columbia University, with the intention of returning to the financial industry after graduation. In her final year, she took a class in which she had to invent a business and write a launch plan for it. "I was already doing a lot of needlepoint, so I decided to use my hobby as the basis for my business plan," Amy says. "Since it was so difficult to find projects that appealed to my urban lifestyle in New York, I felt there was an unmet need for a new style of needlepoint kits."

After researching and evaluating the craft industry, Amy realized that needlepoint could produce not just a theoretical business, but a real one. But even with an MBA in hand, she was unprepared. "I had no contacts, no mentor, little money, and only this vague idea of how I'd produce and sell my needlepoint kits." A poll of her peers revealed that most women in their twenties and thirties don't know how to needlepoint, so Amy decided to target her first kit to a beginner, incorporating a contemporary style that would appeal to grown-ups. Once it was ready, Amy signed up as a vendor at small venues that sold hip crafts to the general public. This process helped her better determine how her kit would be received by retail customers.

As Amy prepared to exhibit at her first major trade show, she had a stroke of marketing genius. Her kit was featured in a needlepoint class in advance of the show, so when her booth opened Amy had a stampede of twenty enthusiastic customers. Amy was on her way. She spent the better part of the next year building her own online store at www.amhdesignonline.com. "I recognized that wholesale business to needlepoint stores would not provide enough volume to grow my business, so I decided to sell directly to retail customers," she says. "This is not a popular idea in the needlepoint world, but it has been a great vehicle for sales as well as press mentions in fashion/home décor magazines and online outlets like DailyCandy."

Although Amy's talent is lucrative, she describes her life as hectic. "I am still doing more jobs than I can properly handle because I'm too busy to hire someone to help me be less busy. Plus, no one will put as much time, care, or effort into my business as I will." She spends her days filling orders from her trade shows, designing new kits and writing instruction manuals for them, invoicing, and ordering supplies. And in all of her spare time, Amy is working on a needlepoint book. "I haven't had a vacation in six months," she confesses.

Amy may have started out as a gifted needlepoint artist, but she has become an expert salesperson. "I've learned that people like to have choices, but too many choices will confuse them, so you need to find the sweet spot for how many product variations to offer," she says. "Also, people don't have a lot of imagination when it comes to understanding how something will look, so if you are showing a sample at a trade show, make sure it's as close to the final product as possible."

Amy has optimistic advice for the would-be artists of the world. "I think it's best to be a bit naïve starting out, and to go into an area where you don't have any prior work experience. That way, you don't have any preconceived notions, you don't know what the status quo is in the industry, and you don't necessarily have to do things the way everyone else has been doing them forever." She does caution those with talent to be realistic about the transition they're about to undertake. "It's going to take longer than you expect and cost more money than you planned, and you will most likely have to make some lifestyle adjustments. But when it works out, being your own boss is fantastic!"

Jonathan
From Painter to Chef

Growing up in Smithville, a small town in Missouri just north of Kansas City, Jonathan demonstrated a gift for painting. Much to the dismay of his highly educated parents, Jonathan's high school art teacher encouraged him to apply to the well-known Art Center College of Design in Pasadena, California. Jonathan was accepted and began studying illustration and abstract and contemporary painting. Although the school has a 40 percent drop out rate, Jonathan made it through. "Being at the Art Center instilled in me an extremely strong work ethic and an almost obsessive attention to detail," he says. In no time, Jonathan was living the starving-artist lifestyle in San Francisco. "I worked as a bike messenger for a while, repossessed cars. I actually met my wife while hanging out in the coolest biker bar in San Francisco, Casa Loma. It was owned by some East Indian guys and had a bunch of transvestite employees left over from the former establishment. What a time that was!"

Jonathan landed a few gallery shows here and there, but he needed to pay his rent so he took a job doing design work for Paul

Ma architects. There he made models and prototypes of resorts, restaurants, and retail shops from wood and metals. He was hard at work as an architectural designer when he landed his first solo gallery show. "I needed to focus, so my wife and I moved to the south of France to prepare," Jonathan remembers. "Unfortunately, when we were ready to come back to the States, we couldn't afford a place in San Francisco." And despite the success of his first major show, Jonathan couldn't muster much enthusiasm for painting. "You put in long, long hours as an artist, and it's a very solitary lifestyle. I'm a social person and it was a little depressing."

At the same time, Jonathan was becoming a serious cook. He had grown up in a cooking family and his older brother was a professional chef. "I recall being four years old and standing at the stove on a step stool making eggs," he says. "My wife and I always blew our paychecks eating out at the best restaurants, and we talked occasionally about opening a restaurant. When painting no longer interested me, I began to notice that the composition of food consists of five elements. It's similar to the color wheel, and designing a plate is much like creating a painting." Jonathan and his wife returned to Jonathan's birthplace of Smithville, and purchased a hundred year-old Montgomery Ward catalog house for the price of a used car.

Then, one night at the age of thirty-two, Jonathan was eating at a restaurant, Le Fou Frog, in Kansas City. "I was absolutely blown away by the food, so I told the chef I wanted to work there and left my number," he says. "When I got home, the phone rang, and it was the chef. He said that I could have a job if I showed up within the next hour." Jonathan hurried back and was rewarded with his first cooking job. He found that he reveled in the camaraderie of the kitchen and was willing to work harder than he had in his life. "I took a huge pay cut, and the chef who hired me was this volcanic guy who was constantly firing me and rehiring me."

Jonathan also came to realize that the chef's world is not as sexy as it appears on television. "You cut and burn yourself, and you work within a structure that's like the military. People on the fringe of society who don't quite fit in anywhere else find a place at the bottom of the restaurant kitchen hierarchy," he explains.

Jonathan eventually left Le Fou Frog, but he was hooked on food. Through the next few years, he took a series of jobs at a food stylist, a meat company, and a fish company—all the while, mastering the chef's competencies. When the time was right, Jonathan decided to open his own restaurant. "We wanted to stay in Missouri so that we could own it outright, and we were able to secure the location of my family's former pharmacy." The new establishment, Justus Drugstore (www.drugstorerestaurant.com), featured "country food on steroids" and was soon one of the most critically acclaimed restaurants in the Kansas City area.

In designing his menu, Jonathan often returns to his painting roots. "I start with a concept and then make each part a reality from there. For example, I remembered root beer from my childhood and wanted to do something with that, so I created this brisket that incorporated root beer milk. It's one of my favorites," he says. On an average day, Jonathan gets up around 11 A.M., speaks with his many suppliers, and forages ingredients from the nearby woods. He'll meet with his sous-chef to determine the day's priorities and coordinate the kitchen's operations. "We have national reviewers coming in now, so every meal is important. In a small kitchen, not one person can be missing. It's like going to war with your comrades every night."

Jonathan is unique in that he transitioned from one tough creative career into an equally competitive one. Yet somehow he has managed to come out on top. "In the food world, it's a huge effort to go from being mediocre to being superb, and my obsessive-compulsive disorder and low self-esteem have allowed me to get there," Jonathan says. "I'm simply not happy unless every detail is perfect and every customer is pleased." Jonathan tells other talented individuals not to let money get in the way, and to stay true to what you want because it may take a while to fully realize your dream. "Do it your own way, because then it's most satisfying."

☞ Self-Reflection: Is Talent Your Motivation?

• Have you honed your talent from a young age?
• Do you believe that your talent, at least in part, defines who you are?

- Have you watched talent competitions on television and genuinely believed you were better than many of the finalists?
- Do most people who witness your talent ask you if you do it for a living?
- Have you heard of others in your situation who have parlayed their talent into careers?
- Have you experienced success exhibiting your talent in unpaid forums?
- Do you have evidence that you would enjoy practicing your talent as a career and not just as a hobby?
- Has anyone ever volunteered to pay you for your talent without you asking?
- Do you sneak off during lunch hour and breaks at work to network on behalf of your talent?
- Do you devote discretionary income to your talent?

👍 If you answered "Yes" to two or more of these questions, you might have a talent that's worth pursuing as a career. Personal talents vary considerably, but in an informal survey of the fields pursued by talented individuals, the seven described in the next section were cited the most. Keep reading for ideas on breaking in.

👉 Putting the Change to Work

A career in visual art: As in many creative fields, it's debatable whether you should get an undergraduate or master's degree if you want to forge a career in painting, drawing, sculpture, photography, or other types of visual art. There are thousands of reputable programs (check out www.allartschools.com) that will certainly provide the technical background you need to refine your craft, but additional schooling does not necessarily ensure your success as a paid artist. What you definitely need, however, is a collection of your best work samples in the form of a portfolio. The design and organization of your portfolio will vary depending on your medium, but make sure that it is clean and professionally produced in both print and online formats. If you can afford it, place the online version in the context of a larger website that contains your biographical and contact information and is easy to find in the search engines. Next, rent or set aside a studio space in your home where you can compile a body of work to be entered in open and juried exhibitions. Become familiar with your local art scene—researching venues where you might sell your work and comparing similar art to accurately assess what you should charge for yours. Attend as many gallery openings as you hear about and meet with the art directors. Once you have something to show, hold your own studio parties, too.

Ini Augustine, president and CEO of ProVision Staffing Group, remarks that visual artists can generate income more quickly by partnering with existing businesses and by cross marketing. "Compile a list of the twenty-five largest companies in your area and offer your services as an artist on projects they may have," she says. In particular, you might have success marketing your services commercially to local painters, builders, remodelers, and designers. "You should also contact your local Chamber of Commerce to find out about trade shows and fairs where you can submit your work. For example, in Minnesota, we have independent artist showings like the St. Paul Art Crawl, and at the state fair, you can rent a booth and sell your art to passersby." Network with other artists and potential customers everywhere you go, and compile an email database of people who are interested in your work. Truly talented artists will amass a following in no time!

A career as a novelist: When people think of talented writers, novelists are usually the first ones to come to mind. Being extraordinarily gifted at fiction writing, though, is both a blessing and a curse, as this world is notoriously hard to break into. The best way to do it is a little at a time while maintaining your job that pays the bills. You can start by perusing bookstores for the type of books you want to write and gaining a comprehensive knowledge of your genre of choice (literary, children's, chick lit, etc.). Test the waters and determine if others recognize your talent by submitting short pieces to writing contests and literary journals such as *Glimmer Train,* those published by McSweeney's, and *Zoetrope: All-Story*. While you work on your first book, join a relevant third-party association such as the Society of Children's Book Writers & Illustrators (www.scbwi.org)

or the American Society of Journalists and Authors (www.asja.org). Attend workshops, conferences, and critique groups so that you can become part of your local writing community and solicit valuable feedback on your book.

Although more and more fiction writers are self-publishing these days, if you want to launch a long-term writing career, you are probably best off going with a traditional publisher, even if small, for your first novel. In order to connect with most editors, you will need to go through a literary agent. Check out sources such as the *Writer's Market* and the *Literary Market Place* to identify agents who represent your type of book, and get referrals from published authors you know. Make sure your targets have solid sales records and charge absolutely no fees besides the standard 15 percent commission. It's standard practice to contact prospective agents via an emailed query letter that stimulates interest in your book. If you're lucky, you will obtain a great agent who will sell your novel to an interested editor. You may then be asked to complete revisions, or you will move directly into the production process. This will likely involve working with copy editors, art designers, sales representatives, and publicity staff to prepare for the publication date. In *The Savvy Author's Guide to Book Publicity*, Lissa Warren suggests collaborating with the publisher's in-house PR staff to develop press materials; send advance copies out for review; pitch print, radio TV, and online media; excerpt content for publication in feature magazines, blogs, or newspapers; and develop an author website. Because it takes a long time to write a novel, keep the momentum up by conceiving your next project as soon as your first has sold. And if the whole publishing process takes longer than you thought, don't despair. Creative writers may also consider careers in journalism, marketing, and copywriting.

A career performing music: While many of the world's visible musicians are in rock bands we see in concert or download on iTunes, those with vocal or instrumental talent actually have an array of career options. Besides becoming a recording artist, you might earn a paycheck as an instrumental soloist, a studio musician, a hotel or restaurant musician, a private function musician, or an orchestra or band member. All working musicians spend large amounts of time rehearsing and perfecting their repertoire, and whichever direction you decide to pursue, you'll need to understand the basics of your area of the business. For instance, one of my friends is a trombone player who manages a brass quintet. Over the last few years, he has had to learn how to get permission to play certain music, how to obtain studio space, and how to distribute a record commercially.

Many people with substantial musical talent wish to gain traction as independent acts. In his article "10 Essential Tips for Making a Living with Your Music," author Christopher Knab advises these folks to create and give away sample CDs and to put their music on websites that allow people to download new music. He encourages them to play often and play for free, offer their services to nonprofit organizations and places of worship, and check out restaurants and clubs where local musicians perform. "As you establish yourself and more and more people show up at your shows, the paid gigs will increase," he writes.

Career musicians must be as creative and passionate about promoting themselves as they are about singing or playing. Develop a professional press kit with short, easy-to-read information on your training, works, appearances, sales, and reviews, and consider hiring a publicist to help you get the word out in the media. If you are looking to publish your music for widespread consumption, research potential labels carefully and hire an attorney to review any contracts before signing them. Once you're doing paid gigs semi-regularly, it may make sense to obtain an experienced manager who can assist with the business side and pursue new recording and publishing deals on your behalf.

A career preparing food: If you look forward to dinnertime so that you can impress your significant other with your culinary powers, or if your friends tell you that your chicken cacciatore beats the neighborhood Italian joint by a mile, why not think about sharing your talent with restaurant patrons? Once you've decided on your specialty and the environment you most enjoy preparing food in, it's time to get out there. While many chefs get their start by attending an independent cooking school, a degree program in culinary arts, or a vocational institute accredited by the American Culinary Federation, others bypass formal education and launch their careers as apprentices to more senior restaurant chefs. Check out your options at www.acfchefs.org, and if you can't get an apprenticeship right away, consider volunteering or working in a noncooking position so that you can see what the daily restaurant grind is like and get to know the kitchen personnel.

Regardless of their education, most chefs start at the bottom of the kitchen hierarchy. You'll likely start out as a line cook who is responsible for a certain aspect of the menu. Once you've demonstrated your talent and willingness to learn, you might become a department specialist who produces a group of foods, and then a sous-chef, who is responsible for behind-the-scenes kitchen management. You may or may not want to reach the highest level of executive chef, for many in this role don't cook as much as they direct.

If you decide that the restaurant world is not for you but you still want to cook for a living, you might consider a career as a caterer or personal chef. Break in by taking a job as an assistant or staffer at a resort, hotel, or catering company. You can also offer to prepare food for your friends' parties, charging them a minimal cost in exchange for distributing business cards on site.

A career in fashion: Many naturally talented designers dream of making it big in the high-profile fashion world. There are a variety of ways into this competitive industry, but many experts agree that attending a prestigious design school such as the Parsons School of Design (www.parsons.edu) or the Pratt Institute (www.pratt.edu) provides the best foundation. In order to be considered for such programs, you will need to create a portfolio of design drawings that demonstrates a unique vision and an understanding of modern fashion sensibilities. A chief advantage of fashion design programs is the opportunity to work alongside world-class designers and to apply for grants that reward your talent.

If you've had enough schooling for the time being, an internship is a terrific way to get hands-on experience and exposure. Contact individual designer showrooms or fashion houses to get information on their programs and review publications like *WWD* for contacts and help-wanted ads. Internships will most likely be compensation free, so get paid in contacts. Make an effort to get to know everyone you work with personally, and ask them to introduce you to other people in the industry who can help drive your career forward.

Some budding fashionistas begin as assistant designers, sample makers, or sketchers for top design houses or mass-market manufacturers, while others launch their own labels right away. If the latter option is what you're after, you must understand the space in which you'll be operating and how you'll produce and market your product. Since you'll need enough money to keep your line afloat for a full year without generating profits, those who are transitioning from another career path would be wise to stay employed and run their fashion enterprise out of their homes in the beginning. Geographic location is another consideration, as it helps to live near the major fashion capitals of New York and Los Angeles because it's easier to meet contacts and attract national distributors. Essential reading for all new designers is *The Apparel Strategist* (www .apparelstrategist.com), a monthly newsletter that helps people start fashion-oriented businesses and offers useful tips on organizing promotional events and getting samples reviewed by the fashion press. Above all, plan carefully, for only talented designers who are also talented entrepreneurs will survive in this business.

A career playing sports: Professional athletes usually begin competing at a young age, when they play on high school and college teams and in amateur tournaments. So if you're in your twenties or thirties and aren't on this path already, it will be difficult to secure a salaried job playing most sports. You can, on the other hand, consider becoming a coach, professional instructor, or sports official. In American public schools, some entry-level positions for coaches or instructors simply require that you have experience playing the sport, although in the public sector those coaches who aren't teachers must get certified by the state. Nearly all start out as assistant coaches and work their way up to head coach jobs or jobs at larger institutions. On the private side, venues such as swimming pools, gyms, summer camps, resorts, ski schools, golf courses, riding stables, and martial arts studios regularly employ talented individuals to teach classes to paying customers. Research the commercial enterprises in your area that focus on your sport, and ask about their requirements for new instructors.

According to the Bureau of Labor Statistics' *Occupational Outlook Handbook*, each sport has specific requirements for umpires, referees, and other sports officials, and these professionals often begin their careers by volunteering for intramural, community, and recreational league competitions. To officiate at high school athletic events, you must register with the state agency that oversees high school athletics and pass an exam on the rules of your particular game. For college refereeing, candidates must be certified by an officiating school and evaluated during a probationary period. Standards for officials become more stringent as the level of competition advances. Whereas umpires for high school baseball only need a high school diploma or its equivalent, twenty-twenty vision, and quick reflexes, those seeking to officiate at minor- or major-league games must attend a professional umpire training school.

If you thought it was impossible to make money playing your sport, think again. As the baby boomers continue to flood the retirement ranks, the demand for private instructors in leisure activities such as golf and tennis is only going to increase. You may even find that after building up a strong reputation, you're able to spin off your own coaching business.

A career in acting: If you want to get into acting but didn't study it in school, here's some good news. Most working actors suggest that studio or community acting classes are more helpful anyway. The most prestigious studios are located in New York and Los Angeles, but even medium-sized towns usually have courses available. In addition to using education to hone your craft, you should constantly seek opportunities to perform. Community theaters and some colleges open their auditions to the public, and while you're making the rounds, you'll get to know other actors in your area. If you're interested in acting in films, get your start by contacting colleges to see if you can be connected with the directors of student projects. Also check out your local film commission. Independent or studio films being shot on location may be in need of extras, and this is a great way to see what life on a Hollywood set is like.

Early in the process, you'll want to get a head shot taken. A head-shot is an eight-by-ten-inch professional photograph that has your acting résumé typed neatly on the back. Because you're more likely to get auditions when you're represented by a talent agent, this will be your next step. Your best bet is to get introduced or referred to agents by people already working in the business (other actors, cast-ing directors, etc.). Once you have a contract, though, don't assume your agent is going to do all the work. You should be reading indus-try trades like *Back Stage* and *Variety* regularly to see what projects are in the works, and who's involved with them.

Talented actors with a marketable look are bound to get work eventually. Even if you make the move to New York or Los Angeles to be closer to the majority of opportunities, anticipate that most of your gigs will be small at first—a commercial here, a walk-on role there. Just a few jobs in, however, you will be expected to join the union associated with your type of work. Film actors, for example, are members of the Screen Actors Guild. Also note that because the average working actor makes just $5K a year, you may have to keep your current job—or get a new one—to help with the bills.

☞ **Exercise: Finding Outlets for Your Talent**

- Survey the scene at your current job. Brainstorm a few ideas for showcasing your talent there.

- List three jobs held by people with your talent. Which one is the most interesting to you, and what training and/or education is required to pursue it?

- Write the names of three people in your network who are currently making a living using your talent. Conduct informational interviews with each of them this month, and write notes on their recommendations for getting started.

- Research public venues where you might display your talent. List three potentials, and contact each to see how you might participate.

- Research contests or competitions you can enter to gain traction for your talent. List three, and contact each to sign up.

- Look online and read your local newspaper to see if there are any third-party associations or groups in your area that focus on your talent. Choose one, commit to attend the next meeting, and write the date, time, and location.

- RSVP to a party hosted by a friend or colleague. Ask if you can perform or exhibit for free. Write your ideas for the event here.

- Interview a handful of people (disqualify close family or friends) who have witnessed your talent in action. Tell them you're considering changing careers and ask them to evaluate your performance. You may want to use an anonymous written form so people don't have to worry about hurting your feelings.

☞ **Resource Toolkit**

Websites

Actingbiz: www.actingbiz.com
Actors, Models & Talent Competition: www.amtcworld.com
Artistsnetwork: www.artistsnetwork.com
Chef2Chef: www.chef2chef.net
Dexigner: www.dexigner.com
Musicians Atlas: www.musiciansatlas.com
Work in Sports: www.workinsports.com
Writer's Digest: www.writersdigest.com

Books

Beyond Talent: Building a Career in Music (Angela Myles Beeching)
Writer's Market (Robert Brewer)
Career Guide for Creative and Unconventional People (Carol Eikleberry and Richard Nelson Bolles)
Managing Your Career in the Sports Industry (Shelly Field)
The Fashion Designer Survival Guide: Start and Run Your Own Fashion Business (Mary Gehlhar and Diane Von Furstenberg)
How'd You Score That Gig? A Guide to the Coolest Careers and How to Get Them (Alexandra Levit)
Talent Is Never Enough: Discover the Choices That Will Take You Beyond Your Talent (John Maxwell)
How to Market and Sell Your Art, Music, Photographs, & Handmade Crafts Online: Turn Your Hobby into a Cash Machine (Lee Rowley)

Afterword

Many people stay in unsatisfying careers because they believe positive change is impossible. Maybe you're at a point where you feel it would be too costly to leave, or you fear starting over in another industry, where you're out of your element. Maybe you're worried that you'll never be able to compete with the masses who are also looking to change careers in light of the poor economy. I hope the stories in this book, which featured individuals who made major career transitions and ended up happier and more successful than they ever imagined, have helped you realize that finding work that fulfills you and meets your needs is completely doable.

Some books on career change focus on celebrities or people who have been unbelievably lucky and enjoy being in the top 1 percent of their profession. In *New Job, New You,* I deliberately excluded these folks. Don't get me wrong, I'm sure they're wonderful people. But I felt it was important to showcase individuals who are just like you and me in order to demonstrate that career change is something of which we're all capable.

While I was conducting my interviews for this book, I was sometimes moved to tears. I wouldn't consider myself an overly emotional person, but my subjects' stories touched something within me. Here were people who made an effort to understand themselves and their own motivations. They overcame obstacles to consciously seek out lines of work that would allow them to create the lives they wanted. In some ways my interviewees couldn't be more different, but the qualities that facilitated their achievements were present across the board.

- **Persistence:** These accomplished career changers chipped away at their new fields a little at a time. They didn't expect an immediate transformation and didn't pressure themselves to overhaul their lives overnight. Even when the time didn't seem right or circumstances swung out of their favor, these individuals never lost sight of the end goal.
- **Courage:** For most of my subjects, it would have been safer and easier to stay in their original careers. Many of their transitions involved substantial financial and emotional risks, yet they proceeded anyway, trusting that the unknown would prove to be better in the long run.
- **Self-confidence:** Even if they occasionally doubted their abilities, more often my interviewees reminded themselves that they would eventually emerge victorious in their new careers. Their self-confidence was contagious and inspired other people to have faith in them, too.
- **Business savvy:** Whether their new profession involved owning their own enterprise or not, most of my career changers could find their way around a profit-and-loss statement. Either via self-training or schooling, they acquired the knowledge to understand what the market needs and how they could use their unique set of skills and talents to provide it.

My interviewees' stories and advice, as well as the additional research I completed for the book, have led me to think of my own career change from marketing communications executive to author and speaker in a slightly different light. I've recognized how lucky I am to be naturally driven, and someone who finds quitting distasteful. I appreciate my corporate background more than ever, for I see that many of the skills I developed to thrive there apply significantly now that I'm on my own. I've also realized, though, that in the past my lack of self-assurance may have held me back a bit, and that perhaps I don't have to be quite so careful and measured in my next career move. I can watch and plan and tiptoe all I want, but at some point I'll need to trust my instincts and jump. Where will your career take you, and where will mine take me? We'll just have to wait and see!

Acknowledgments

New Job, New You reflects my evolution as a career advice author and speaker, and it would not have been possible without the assistance of the thirty talented and dynamic individuals profiled within it. Thank you for making us feel like career change is possible for anyone at any time.

Thanks to my agent, Michelle Wolfson, for believing in this project, and my editor, Christina Duffy, for championing it. My terrific team at Random House—Jane von Mehren, Beth Pearson, Tom Pitoniak, Liz Cosgrove, Erin Bekowies—have been proof that the second time's a charm. You've made the process as smooth as can be, and for that I am incredibly grateful.

My sincerest appreciation goes out to the team at *The Wall Street Journal*, especially Jennifer Merritt and David Crook. The "Reinvent" column is a dream come true.

I wouldn't be where I am without the constant support of my husband, Stewart Shankman; my father, Robert Levit; and my dearest friend, Kathryn Mayurnik Sein. I continue to value the guidance and camaraderie of the writers and bloggers in the career space, especially Jason Alba, Diane Danielson, Jason Dorsey, Michelle Goodman, Christine Hassler, Julie Jansen, Lindsey Pollak, Curt Russell, Dan Schawbel, Hannah Seligson, Pamela Slim, Penelope Trunk, and Bruce Tulgan.

To my family, my friends, my readers, and my son's caregiver, Beverly Jackson—it's because of you that I can do what I do every day. Thank you a million times over.

Find Our Career Changers' Businesses

Leslie: www.leslieesdailebanks.com (novels)
J.B.: www.pkolino.com (children's furniture)
Erica: www.momspace.com (online community)
Lisa Marie: www.upsidethinking.com (leadership development)
Kami: www.spacushion.com (spa products)
Ricardo: www.ricompanada.com (empanadas)
Liene: www.blueorchidweddings.com (wedding planning)
Scott: www.expeditionswest.com (adventure travel)
Kim: www.karinnewbygallery.com (art gallery)
Ryan: www.learnfrommylife.com (online community)
Randy: www.leverageagency.com (sponsorships)
Michelle: www.wasabipublicity.com (publicity)
Jonathan: www.jonathangstein.com (personal injury law)
Valerie: www.bigfeetpjs.com (adult pajamas)
Jason: www.jasonmillerphotography.com (photography)
Kate: www.katesclub.org (children's advocacy)
Tara: www.giftedatbirth.com and http://www.powerofbirth.com
   (doula services)
Patrick: www.createyourowndestiny.com (motivational speaking)
Jason: www.jibberjobber.com (career software)
Nicole: www.theadoptionconsultancy.com (adoption services)
Adam: www.junobaby.com (children's educational products)
Jennifer: www.healthandthecity.net (martial arts training)
Amy: www.amhdesignonline.com (needlepoint products)
Jonathan: www.drugstorerestaurant.com (restaurant)

Bibliography

Chapter One: Family

CareerBuilder.com. "CareerBuilder.com Launches CareerPath.com to Connect the More than One-Third of Workers Considering a Career Change with Available Jobs." http://www.prnewswire.com/cgi-bin/stories.pl?ACCT=BPITE.story&STORY=/www/story/08-01-2007/0004637123&EDATE=WED+Aug+01+2007,+10:17+AM. 2007.

Furman, Phyllis. "Balancing Kids and Careers." http://www.nydailynews.com/money/2007/09/17/2007-09-17_balancing_kids_and_careers.html. 2007.

Galinsky, Ellen. "Dual-Centric: A New Concept of Work-Life." http://www.familiesandwork.org/site/research/reports/dual-centric.pdf (accessed 2008).

Gichon, Galia. "7 Financial Steps Every Working Mom Needs to Know." http://www.jobsandmoms.com/gichonarticle.html (accessed 2009).

Goodman, Michelle. *My So-Called Freelance Life: How to Survive and Thrive as a Creative Professional for Hire*. Berkeley, Calif.: Seal, 2008.

Gordon, Gil, and Work & Family Connection. "Making Telecommuting Successful: A Guide for Employees." http://www.jobsandmoms.com/want_to_telecommute.html (accessed 2009).

Johnson, Tory. "Tory Johnson's Tips to Make Money at Home." http://abcnews.go.com/GMA/AsSeenOnGMA/story?id=4585337&page=1. 2008.

Mason, Mary Ann, and Eve Mason Ekman. *Mothers on the Fast Track: How a New Generation Can Balance Family and Careers*. New York: Oxford University Press, 2007.

U.S. Bureau of Labor Statistics Occupational Outlook Handbook.

"Teachers: Preschool, Kindergarten, Elementary, Middle, and Secondary." http://www.bls.gov/oco/ocos069.htm. 2008.

U.S. Bureau of Labor Statistics Occupational Outlook Handbook. "Physical Therapists." http://www.bls.gov/oco/ocos080.htm. 2008.

Wilbert, Caroline. "The Six Best Careers for Moms." http://www.divine caroline.com/article/22306/41991-six-careers-moms (accessed 2009).

Chapter Two: Independence

Entrepreneur. "How to Start a Retail Store" (specialty publication) http://www.entrepreneur.com. 2005.

Gold, Steven. *Entrepreneur's Notebook: Practical Advice for Starting a New Business Venture.* Stanford, Calif.: Learning Ventures, 2008.

Goodman, Michelle. *My So-Called Freelance Life: How to Survive and Thrive as a Creative Professional for Hire.* Berkeley, Calif.: Seal, 2008.

Skillings, Pamela. *Escape from Corporate America: A Practical Guide to Creating the Career of Your Dreams.* New York: Ballantine, 2008.

Sloan, Jeff, and Rich Sloan. "10 Steps to Open for Business." http://www.startupnation.com/NET_ROOT/print_template/PrintContent.aspx?content_id=3759 (accessed 2009).

U.S. Small Business Administration Office of Advocacy. "Frequently Asked Questions." http://www.sba.gov/advo/stats/sbfaq.pdf (accessed 2009).

Chapter Three: Learning

Back to College. "Going Back to College: Frequently Asked Questions." http://www.back2college.com/library/faq.htm (accessed 2009).

Back to College. "How to Accelerate Your Degree Plan." http://www.back2college.com/accelerate.htm (accessed 2009).

Kuther, Tara. "Preparation and Your Graduate Admissions Essay." http://gradschool.about.com/cs/essaywriting/a/essay1.htm (accessed 2009).

———. "What Are the Common Topics for Graduate School Admissions Essays?" http://gradschool.about.com/od/essaywriting/f/essay2.htm (accessed 2009).

MsMoney.com. "What to Look for in a Business School." http://www.msmoney.com/mm/career/backto_school/business_schools.htm (accessed 2009).

Siebert, A, and Karr, Mary. *The Adult Student's Guide to Survival and Success.* Portland, Ore.: Practical Psychology, 2003.

Chapter Four: Money

Back to College. "Going Back to College: Frequently Asked Questions." http://www.back2college.com/library/faq.htm (accessed 2009).

Cowan, Kristina. "Top Paying Jobs in America—IT, Finance Industries Lead the Way." http://blogs.payscale.com/content/2008/01/top-paying-jobs.html. 2008.

Kaufmann, Steve. "Four Steps That Will Improve Your Earning Potential." http://www.dumblittleman.com/2008/02/increase-your-earning-potential.html. 2008.

Heathfield, Susan. "How to Make More Money: Your Lifetime Income Potential." http://humanresources.about.com/od/salaryandbenefits/a/life_earnings.htm (accessed 2009).

Moss, Wes. *Make More, Worry Less: Secrets from 18 Extraordinary People Who Created a Bigger Income and a Better Life.* Upper Saddle River, N.J.: Pearson Education, 2008.

Roth, J. D. "How to Get Out of Debt." http://getrichslowly.org/blog/2006/11/16/how-to-get-out-of-debt-2/. 2006.

Stevenson, Betsey, and Justin Wolfers. "Economic Growth and Subjective Well-Being: Reassessing the Easterlin Paradox." http://bpp.wharton.upenn.edu/betseys/papers/Happiness.pdf. 2008.

Chapter Five: Passion

Chang, Richard. *The Passion Plan.* San Francisco: Jossey-Bass, 2001.

Intuit. "Growth During Recession? Small Businesses Say 'Yes!' Intuit Survey Reveals Small Businesses Bullish on Growth, Despite Economy." http://eon.businesswire.com/portal/site/eon/permalink/?ndmViewId=news_view&newsId=20080403105216&newsLang=en. 2008.

Money. "Money Magazine Releases Second Annual Report on the Best Jobs in America: Exclusive List Developed with Salary.com to Find the Best 'Second Act' Careers." http://www.timeinc.net/fortune/information/presscenter/money/press_releases/20070322_bestjobs_MON.html. 2007.

Rosengren, Curt. "Start Now: Inject Your Career with More Passion Through These Six Steps." http://www.passioncatalyst.com/media/6steps.pdf. 2004.

Siciliano, Tom, and Jeff Caliguire. *Shifting into Higher Gear: An Owner's Manual for Uniting Your Calling and Career.* San Francisco: Jossey-Bass, 2005.

Chapter Six: Setback

Kübler-Ross, Elisabeth. *On Death and Dying.* New York: Scribner, 1997.

Ma, Lybi. "Down but Not Out." http://www.psychologytoday.com/articles/pto-20040329-000005.html. 2004.

Manz, Charles. *The Power of Failure: 27 Ways to Turn Life's Setbacks into Success*. San Francisco: Berrett-Koehler, 2002.

Richardson, Bradley. *Regaining Your Confidence After a Big Career Setback*. http://online.wsj.com/article/SB120827184547116311.html? mod=googlenews_wsj. 2004.

Chapter Seven: Talent

Augustine, Ini. "How to Make Money as an Artist." http://www.ehow .com/how_2170221_money-as-artist.html (accessed 2009).

Knab, Christopher. "10 Essential Tips for Making a Living with Your Music." http://www.musicbizacademy.com/knab/articles/ 10makealiving.htm. 2004.

National Endowment for the Arts. "National Endowment for the Arts Announces New" *Artists in the Workforce* Study. http://www.nea.gov/ news/news08/ArtistsinWorkforce.html. 2008.

Stanton, Aaron. "What Are the Odds of Succeeding at Outlandish Dreams?" http://beta.booklamp.org/forum/index.php/ topic,189.0.html. 2008.

U.S. Bureau of Labor Statistics Occupational Outlook Handbook. "Athletes, Coaches, Umpires, and Related Workers." http://www.bls .gov/oco/ocos251.htm. 2008.

Warren, Lissa. *The Savvy Author's Guide to Book Publicity*. New York: Carroll & Graf, 2004.

Alexandra Levit is a nationally recognized business and workplace author and speaker. A syndicated columnist for *The Wall Street Journal* and *Metro US*, Levit has authored several books, including the popular *They Don't Teach Corporate in College, How'd You Score That Gig?*, and *Success for Hire.*

Levit makes frequent national media appearances and has been featured in thousands of outlets including *The New York Times, USA Today,* National Public Radio, ABC News, Fox News, CNBC, the Associated Press, *Glamour, Cosmopolitan,* and *Fortune,* and her articles regularly appear on the home pages of CNN, MSN, and Yahoo!.

Known as one of the premier spokespeople of her generation, Levit regularly speaks at conferences, universities, and corporations—including Campbell's Soup, CIGNA, the Federal Reserve Bank, McDonald's, and Whirlpool—on issues facing modern employees. She is also a global spokesperson for Microsoft and has recently been called upon to speak to baby-boomer and Generation X managers about leveraging the talent of the Millennial Generation.

Levit recently served on a committee that advised the Obama administration on workplace developments. She has ten years of experience providing integrated marketing communications solutions for Fortune 500 companies and is also skilled at providing guidance regarding twenty-first-century motherhood, human resources and general business issues, and entrepreneurship. She graduated from Northwestern University and resides in Chicago with her husband, Stewart, and their son, Jonah.